THE ART OF COLLECTIVE BARGAINING

THE ART OF COLLECTIVE BARGAINING

SECOND EDITION

JOHN P. SANDERSON, Q.C.

1989
CANADA LAW BOOK INC.
240 EDWARD STREET, AURORA, ONTARIO

© 1989
CANADA LAW BOOK INC.

Canadian Cataloguing in Publication Data

Sanderson, John P.
    The art of collective bargaining

2nd ed.
Includes bibliographical references.
ISBN 0-88804-069-5

1. Collective bargaining. 2. Collective bargaining —
Canada. I. Title.

KE0645.S36 1989   331.89   C89-094977-8
KF3408.S36 1989

Acknowledgments

This new edition is, I think, a better book than its predecessor. Part of the reason is that I have learned much in my recent negotiating travels. More importantly, I have had the benefit of many helpful comments and observations from other practitioners of the art of collective bargaining, both labour and management. I am grateful to all of them and I hope I have adequately captured their particular concerns.

I also want to acknowledge and pay tribute to the editing talents of two of my colleagues in my law practice, Heather Laing and Maureen Farson. Their help has been invaluable and the book has been improved by them. My secretary, who had the tiresome task of assembling the various drafts of the manuscript, has insisted she not be named or have her large contribution recognized, so I will not do so.

Finally, if I may be briefly personal, this new book would not have been written — nor could it have been written — if it were not for my wife and what she has given me.

Toronto, Ontario   John P. Sanderson, Q.C.
May 1989

Prologue

Sitting in his living room late one night, with the first collective bargaining meeting he'd ever attended due to start at 9:30 the next morning, with him in charge of the Company team — some team, him and a part-time accountant — Don Lucas was not at peace with the world. Indeed, Don was more than a little unhappy, at least with what had happened to Lucas Manufacturing.

You see, the Company and Don were one and the same; at least that's how Don figured it. It made sense. Fifteen years ago Don, the local bank manager and Don's retired father-in-law put together a mix of ideas, money, knowledge and enthusiasm, and the good ship Lucas was launched, not into a sea of prosperity, but more a pond of survivability. For some years it staggered along, from one bank overdraft crisis to another. Then salvation came, sort of. One of the auto companies placed a small order, then increased it a little more, and Don was hooked. New equipment, more employees, larger debt, increased work pace, deadlines, penalty clauses, headaches at business and home — all those good things that go with growth and progress.

But now Don was scared. A union, the United Workers of North America, had been granted the exclusive right to represent his employees at the plant. His employees! Bringing in a union! How could they do this to him, after all he had done for them? Now only Don and his foreman were not covered by the certification order. At least, that's what he thought it said.

Would the union let him keep operating? What could he do if it decided to crush him and his little business? "What infuriates me", he thought, "is that I've lost control. The Company is no longer mine. It's the goddam union's. I want to fight, but if there's a strike the auto company will pull their tooling, and I'm down the tubes financially. But, will my people go on strike? I never thought they'd think of a union, much less get one in here. Guess I can't call them my people any more."

"And what about all this bargaining stuff? I'm sure not going to give away the Company. I wish I knew what to ask for, but I guess I'll have to wait until tomorrow to see what the union wants. I can always just tell them no, let them try to run the Company. I wonder who'll be there. I heard something about Mary Anne Mosley being the leader for the union."

On a another street in the same town, Mary Anne sat in her blue housecoat at the kitchen table, sipping tea, while her cat rubbed against her ankles. "Damn, how did I end up as Chair of the union bargaining committee at the plant?", she wondered. "For thirteen years I've worked as an assembler, then an inspector, doing my job as best I could. It's not been a bad job, but not good either. Especially now, ever since the automobile contract. Everyone — Don particularly — got so excited at first. Didn't they know what it would mean? God, it used to be so relaxed, people even smiled at work. They cared. Now it's push, push, at me, at everyone, to get the stuff out, get the boxes filled and onto the trucks and out to the customers. Everyone yells for more, no matter how hard you try. We're all fed up."

"But me and the kids need this job. Especially the kids. Their father — wherever he is — couldn't care less, so it's up to me to keep them going. Maybe the union will help. They say they can. Their papers and their leaflets sound pretty good. But I don't know about this strike business. There's nothing in my bank account. What will the kids and I live on? No one's ever helped me out before. Why should I trust them?"

"And what is this bargaining business anyway? Who are we bargaining for — the union, or us? And what is supposed to go into a collective agreement? What does it say? Anyway, I'm glad the union is sending in a negotiator, a real pro. I can't wait to see him go after Don. He's not a bad guy, but he can be a real smart-ass sometimes. He seems to think even the toilet paper belongs to him! Besides, his wife is the best-dressed woman in town, and she's never worked a day in her life. It's just not fair. What's the union guy's name again — oh, John R. Franklin."

John R. Franklin, Rob to his friends, has just checked into the Sunburst Motel, worn, tired, and more than a little bit concerned. Tomorrow bargaining starts at Lucas Manufacturing, and 'yours truly' is leading the union team! Fearless he is not. Tony Orsini, the union's Director of Organizing and usual negotiator of first collective agreements in this region, had just suffered his second heart attack. Too much stress, smoke, booze and late nights — nothing unusual. Sounds like a bypass, maybe a triple or more. Rob was the replacement negotiator, two years from college, dragged screaming out of his research office and sent out to bargain in the field; some town he'd never heard of, could hardly even find on the map. A first-time bargainer, leaving behind his computer, his print-outs, a world clean and ordered, like the numbers that marched in neat lines up and down the pages, doing wondrous things that only he could understand. And now he had to jump in cold into the negotiating water. At least he'd taken a course the union had put on about bargaining. What was it that hot-shot had said about negotiating? Oh yes, I remember; "Negotiating is like sex. You only learn about it by doing it."

This book is written for Don, for Mary Anne, for Rob, for all those persons who have not yet been there while the negotiating universe unfolds — not necessarily as it should.

Table of Contents

Chapter 1

Introduction

The term "collective agreement" is a term of art. If you are an employee covered by a collective agreement, it tells you the rate of pay for your job and describes your working conditions and benefits. More narrowly, a collective agreement is an agreement in writing between an employer or group of employers and a union or council of unions which contains provisions about the terms and conditions of employment of employees covered by the collective agreement.

In a general sense, a collective agreement is a collection of commitments in writing by an employer, a union and a group of employees to do certain things and not to do certain other things. It is a document of varying length and complexity which represents the sum of the compromises and the victories and defeats, large and small, between one group of negotiators and the other. It is a political and, at the same time, a legal document. It is a rug under which some matters may be swept to create an illusion that they have been addressed, even if not resolved. More importantly, it is a living record of the continuing relationship between an employer, a union and a group of employees, binding on them all, to be respected or reviled but, in any event, to govern the relationship of the parties and provide a code of conduct for them to follow and enforce against each other.

A collective agreement does not spring from the earth in final form or arrive by accident. It is created by the efforts and energies of negotiators who struggle to reach unanimity without self-destructing. The collective bargaining process is adversarial in nature and represents a process in which two parties, starting from opposite and competing positions, arrive at a cease-fire arrangement or accommodation for a specific period of time. When a collective agreement expires, the parties then renegotiate the terms to form the next collective agreement.

Collective bargaining is not, in a phrase, a group of persons sitting down "to reason together". More accurately, collective bargaining is an example of applied politics, a means to reach a result, namely, the resolution or suspension of competing interests for the length of time covered by the collective agreement. It is an opportunity for negotiators for an employer and a union to discuss mutual problems, concerns and priorities, and to fashion

1

appropriate compromises and solutions. The collective bargaining process is itself neutral and it is only invested with life and substance when people, called negotiators, begin to interact and react at the bargaining table.

1. Establishment of a Collective Bargaining Relationship

Why do the parties have to bargain? Who says they must? There are two ways in which a collective bargaining relationship is created. The first, and by far the most common way, is through certification. A union applies to the labour relations board in the province in which it does business or, if it is federally regulated, to the Canada Labour Relations Board, on behalf of a group of employees that it represents. Subject to the representation requirements of that board, the union will receive a certificate of representation which designates the union as the sole and exclusive collective bargaining agent of the employees in a described bargaining unit. Certification by a labour board imposes on the union and the employer a statutory obligation to meet together, to bargain in good faith and to make every reasonable effort to reach a collective agreement. Some of the intricacies and interpretations of what is meant by "bargaining in good faith" are dealt with in a later chapter. It is sufficient at this point to recognize that the concept has both subjective and objective elements.

The second way in which a collective bargaining relationship is established occurs when an employer voluntarily recognizes a union as the bargaining agent for certain identifiable employees. In most jurisdictions, an employer may choose to recognize a union, but if it does so it must outline this intention in writing for it to be binding. In this case, the recognition document must designate or identify the group of employees for which the union has been recognized by the employer as the bargaining agent. In some jurisdictions, however, there is a statutory requirement upon the parties to a first collective agreement made as a result of voluntary recognition to establish, if challenged, that at the time voluntary recognition was granted a majority of the employees in the bargaining unit were members of the union.

The practical effect of the imposition of this statutory requirement is that any person, which obviously includes another union or any individual employee, may challenge the first collective agreement reached by the parties to a voluntary recognition agreement. If such a challenge is made, the parties to that collective agreement are obliged to produce evidence that the union represented a majority of the employees at the point in time when the employer granted the voluntary recognition agreement to the union. To protect themselves, some parties to a voluntary recognition agreement have arranged for membership cards or other documentation designating union membership to be produced to an independent third party, who in turn counts and authenticates such membership documents. A statement from this person can be filed as appropriate evidence that the union was selected by a majority of the employees in the bargaining unit. In any case, this statutory provision applies only during the first year of the first collective agreement that the parties negotiate. After the first year, that collective agreement is treated no differently than any other collective agreement which has been reached as a result of the certification procedure.

While there are exceptions, the vast majority of collective agreements entered into by employers and unions are reached after certification and not as a result of voluntary recognition. Both employers and unions have a political interest in protecting themselves against allegations of sweetheart deals without knowing what the employees want, and the best way to ensure this is to shelter behind the protection of a certification order. Most employers, if approached by a union that wants voluntary recognition, will insist that the union proceed through the ordinary channels of the certification procedure. If there is a statutory scheme in Canada regulated by an independent tribunal — as there is — it makes good sense to use it, and to insist that others use it as well.

2. Subjects for Collective Bargaining

A collective agreement must be in written form, and it must contain provisions that set out the terms and conditions of employment. Obviously, any particular collective agreement will include a widely varying range of different subjects and items, including some or all of the respective obligations of an employer, its employees and their union.

While the line between them is blurred, the subjects of collective bargaining can be grouped into two rough columns headed "economic" and "non-economic". For example, the terms of a particular management rights article have major economic consequences on an employer's right to manage its business. The management rights article lists the kinds of decisions to be made solely by the employer in running an operation. Similarly, an article may specify certain limitations or restrictions upon such rights. Nevertheless, there are no precise dollar figures that can be calculated in the abstract as necessarily flowing from agreement or non-agreement to a management rights article, in whatever form it appears. A management rights article is therefore considered to be a non-economic matter.

By the same token, the application of seniority in lay-off situations is of vital importance to all of the parties to a collective agreement, in both human and economic terms. Over time, the way lay-offs are handled, who stays, who goes and in what order, may be as important to the success or failure of the business as the wage schedule itself. However, since the application of a particular seniority arrangement cannot be estimated before lay-offs occur, a seniority issue, like management rights, is normally characterized by most negotiators as a non-economic subject. There is nothing magical in this approach. The use of labels, if consistently applied, brings some order to a process that can be chaotic. System, analysis and structure are as necessary and useful to this process as to any other part of a business.

(a) Mandatory provisions

(i) *Recognition*

Apart from dividing the matters dealt with by collective agreements into economic and non-economic issues, the labour relations statutes identify certain provisions that must be contained in every collective agreement. In all cases, a collective agreement must contain a recognition article, which identifies the group of employees who are bound by the terms of a collective agreement and for whom the union in question has bargained a particular deal. A typical recognition clause would describe a bargaining unit in the same words as the bargaining unit description in the certification order issued by the appropriate labour relations board to a union. For example, the clause might read as follows:

The employer recognizes the union as the sole collective bargaining agent for all its employees employed in Sudbury, save and except forepersons, persons above the rank of foreperson, office and sales staff, and students employed during the school vacation period.

There is no legal obligation on the parties to restrict the wording of a recognition article to the precise unit or bargaining constituency set out in a certification order. More narrowly, the parties may agree to add to or delete some or all of the exclusions found by the labour relations board to be outside the bargaining unit and therefore not covered by a collective agreement. For instance, in the example cited, the parties might decide to add to the list of exclusions another category, namely truck drivers, perhaps on the grounds that the drivers have few common employment interests with the plant employees who work inside in contrast to being out on the road all day every day. The parties may also word a recognition clause to change the geographical limitations imposed by the board in the certification order, either by contracting the geographical boundaries to part of a city or community or by extending them to cover an entire province or country.

In most jurisdictions, the practice has been for a certificate to be directed to a particular work location, so that those employees who are covered by a certification order and for whom a union has established its representation rights can be clearly identified. Thus, a union is normally granted certification for the employees in an appropriate bargaining unit at a specific location where those same employees work, or at least report for work. This is not a problem where an employer has only one operation, but different consider-ations arise where an employer has other facilities or operations in other locations.

If a collective agreement contains a recognition article which omits the restriction to a defined geographical area such as "employees employed in the City of Brockville", and directly or indirectly covers all employees of that employer in Ontario, the parties may have constructed a labour relations land-mine for themselves, for they have entered into what amounts to a voluntary recognition agreement covering all of the employer's plants located in cities outside of Brockville. This would mean that the union would have bargaining rights at these locations without using the certification procedure and, perhaps, without the endorsement or even awareness of the employees at those locations. If employees have the right to select a union of their choice to represent them in collective bargaining with their employer — and the law gives them this right — it follows they must be given the knowledge and the opportunity to make such a choice, rather than have a union imposed on them by the action of the respective pens of their employer and the union.

In addition to this legalistic concern, there is a compelling practical reason for the parties to restrict a recognition article to the certification order. It is a cornerstone of the labour relations legislation that a union must establish, by appropriate evidence of membership, its entitlement to represent an identifiable group of employees who have the same community of interest. If a recognition article is significantly broader and covers more persons at different locations than the group for which a union has been certified as the bargaining agent, both the union and the employer would be open to challenge and criticism. Any person could argue that the union was not chosen by the employees as their own bargaining agent, and had been imposed on them by the private agreement of the employer and the union.

The parties may also frame a recognition clause to exclude certain persons from a bargaining unit. For example, there may be employees who are excluded by the terms of a certification order, but during collective bargaining the parties may conclude that such employees should, in fact, be included in the unit. The reverse may also be true. A particular classification may be in the unit, but the parties may decide to add it to the list of exclusions. There is nothing improper about agreeing to a recognition article that varies the exclusions in a certification order, provided of course that the parties have in fact agreed on what classifications are to be covered by a collective agreement or excluded from it.

The parties still have to put together language that clearly and accurately spells out what has been agreed. Parties that negotiate and reach an agreement in principle stop there at their peril! They have another step to take, namely, to find the right words to reflect the provisions they have negotiated.

(ii) *Grievance and arbitration*

Labour relations legislation also requires the parties to agree upon a method for the final and binding settlement by arbitration of any differences between the parties arising from the interpretation, application, administration or alleged violation of a collective agreement. This kind of provision is normally described as a grievance and arbitration article. If the parties to a collective agreement are unable or unwilling to agree on a procedure for the final settlement of their collective bargaining differences by arbitration, their collective agreement is nevertheless considered to contain such a provision; that is to say, the statute imposes a contractual article upon them. By way of illustration, the appropriate section of the Ontario *Labour Relations Act*, which has its companion across the legislative landscape of Canada, reads as follows:

44.(2) If a collective agreement does not contain such a provision as is mentioned in subsection (1), it shall be deemed to contain the following provision:

Where a difference arises between the parties relating to the interpretation, application or administration of this agreement, including any question as to whether a matter is arbitrable, or where an allegation is made that this agreement has been violated, either of the parties may, after exhausting any grievance procedure established by this agreement, notify the other party in writing of its desire to submit the difference or allegation to arbitration and the notice shall contain the name of the first party's appointee to an arbitration board. The recipient of the notice shall within five days inform the other party of the name of its appointee to the arbitration board. The two appointees so selected shall, within five days of the appointment of the second of them, appoint a third person who shall be the chairman. If the recipient of the notice fails to appoint an arbitrator, or if the two appointees fail to agree upon a chairman within the time limited, the appointment shall be made by the Minister of Labour for Ontario upon the request of either party. The arbitration board shall hear and determine the difference or allegation and shall issue a decision and the decision is final and binding upon the parties and upon any employee or employer affected by it. The decision of a majority is the decision of the arbitration board, but if there is no majority the decision of the chairman governs.

The mechanics for enforcing these kinds of statutory requirements are relatively straightforward. If an issue arises about which a collective agreement is silent, or where the article is inadequate and does not meet the legislative standard, the particular labour relations board may be requested by either party to a collective agreement to amend the collective agreement so as to comply with the statute and provide the requisite arbitration mechanism.

In most collective agreements, there are two separate but connected matters to be addressed in the handling and processing of a grievance to arbitration. The first concerns a procedure which establishes how grievances may be filed. This normally sets out the various stages through which a grievance must proceed, in ascending order, involving increasingly more senior members of the corporate and union hierarchy. The statute does not, however, provide any specific direction about the structure or form of the mechanism the parties may create to handle and, hopefully, resolve the grievance. The second matter, arbitration, becomes an issue only after the parties themselves have tried and failed to settle a particular grievance between themselves. This normally details the manner by which the grieving party obtains a neutral third party, called an arbitrator, to decide the merits of the issue that brought about the grievance.

While the subject will be discussed in more detail in a subsequent chapter, a typical grievance article would read as follows:

.01 The parties to this agreement are agreed that it is of the utmost importance to adjust complaints and grievances concerning the interpretation or alleged violation of the agreement as quickly as possible.

.02 No grievance shall be considered where the events giving rise to it occurred or originated more than two (2) full working days before the filing of the grievance.

.03 Grievances properly arising under this agreement shall be adjusted and settled as follows:

Step No. 1 — The aggrieved employee shall present the grievance orally or in writing to the foreperson. The aggrieved employee shall have the assistance of a steward if so desired. The foreperson shall give a decision within two (2) working days following the presentation of the grievance to the foreperson. If the foreperson's decision is not satisfactory to the employee concerned, then the grievance may be presented as follows:

Step No. 2 — Within two (2) working days after the decision is given at Step No. 1, the aggrieved employee may, with or without the steward, present the grievance (which shall be reduced to writing on a form supplied by the union and approved by the employer) to the Plant Manager, who shall consider it in the presence of the person or persons presenting same and the foreperson, and render a decision in writing within two (2) working days following the presentation of the grievance to the Plant Manager. If a settlement satisfactory to the employee concerned is not reached, then the grievance may be presented as follows:

Step No. 3 — Within two (2) working days after the decision is given under Step No. 2, the aggrieved employee may submit the grievance to the General Manager, and the employee, accompanied by the chair of the Plant Committee and the steward, shall meet as promptly as possible with such persons as the employer may desire, to consider the grievance. At this stage they may be accompanied by a full-time representative of the union if requested by either party. The General Manager will render a decision in writing within two (2) working days following such meeting.

.04 If final settlement of the grievance is not reached at Step No. 3, and if the grievance is one which concerns the interpretation or alleged violation of the agreement, then the grievance may be referred in writing by either party to a board of arbitration as provided in Article VI (Arbitration) below at any time within twenty-one (21) calendar days after the decision is given under Step No. 3, and if no such written request for arbitration is received within the time limited, then it shall be deemed to have been abandoned.

As far as the arbitration stage is concerned, the parties to a collective agreement are free to negotiate an arbitration provision that suits their particular needs, provided that it at least equals the minimum standard set out in the particular labour relations statute that governs their labour relations affairs. More precisely, the provisions must include an arbitration mechanism, a method of selection of an arbitrator, and a commitment that the decision of the arbitrator is final and binding on the parties to the collective agreement. While there are many ways to draft an arbitration provision, the following is an example:

.01 Both parties to this agreement agree that any dispute or grievance concerning the interpretation or alleged violation of this agreement, which has been properly carried through all the steps of the grievance procedure outlined in Article V (Grievance Procedure) above, and which has not been settled, will be referred to a board of arbitration, at the written request of either of the parties hereto.

.02 The board of arbitration will be composed of one (1) person appointed by the employer, one (1) person appointed by the union, and a third person to act as chair chosen by the other two (2) members of the board.

.03 Within five (5) working days of the request by either party for a board, each party shall notify the other in writing of the name of its appointee.

.04 Should the person chosen by the employer to act on the board, and the person chosen by the union, fail to agree on a third person within seven (7) days of the notification mentioned in .03 above, the Minister of Labour of the Province of Ontario may be asked to nominate a person to act as chair at any time thereafter.

.05 The decision of a board of arbitration, or a majority thereof, constituted in the above manner, shall be binding on both parties.

.06 The board of arbitration shall not have any power to alter or change any of the provisions of this agreement or to substitute any new provisions for any existing provisions, or to give any decision inconsistent with the terms and provisions of this agreement.

.07 Each of the parties to this agreement will bear the expenses of the arbitrator appointed by it; and the parties will jointly bear the expenses, if any, of the chair.

This sample provision, as well as the statutory model, establishes that a three-person board of arbitration will be the deciding body or tribunal. By contrast, a number of collective agreements provide for a sole arbitrator to be the decision maker, either in all cases or in specific kinds of grievances. For example, a collective agreement may provide for a single arbitrator to decide discharge and discipline cases, and a three-person board to hear all other grievances. It is to be emphasized that the notion of a single arbitrator is simply a matter of negotiating choice and is not in any way contrary to the statute.

In Ontario, there is another consideration. Prior to 1980, the parties controlled their own arbitration world, except for the construction industry. At that time the legislature created a separate arbitration mechanism by amending the Ontario *Labour Relations Act*. Under a provision of that Act, either party to a collective agreement may elect to ignore the arbitration mechanism that the parties have contractually agreed to use, and may request the government to choose an arbitrator. It does not matter whether the other party agrees or disapproves; this election of a sole arbitrator chosen by the Ministry of Labour is unilateral.

The significance of this to a negotiator is considerable. The Act requires the parties to negotiate an arbitration system that reflects their own priorities and concerns. The Act further provides that all the terms and provisions of the collective agreement are binding on all the parties to it. Yet the same Act also provides that either party, when it suits its purposes, may simply ignore what it has agreed on, and may use statute to secure an arbitrator.

There are at least two difficulties with this approach. The first, in a sense, is philosophical. If the parties have no control over the system, and therefore no vested interest in maintaining responsibility for it, they will not have the same confidence in it. At the same time, they will see no purpose in wasting negotiating time and energy in improving or changing their own arbitration system, since they can always go for the statutory option.

The second difficulty is more subtle and is of more concern. Parties to any collective agreement obtain accord by a series of trade-offs and compromises. Properly, each party applies its own negotiating perspectives and priorities to each issue, and makes adjustments up and down the acceptability scale as the bargaining proceeds. In the end though, the collective agreement they make is their own, and each can leave the bargaining table confident that while it must live up to all of the agreement's terms, so must the other side. Clearly, that is true, except for the arbitration article. That might not matter if it were not for the fact that this article is the enforcement mechanism for the rest of a collective agreement, the means by which differences between the parties are decided in a final and binding manner. An arbitration article in Ontario is effectively a "perhaps" provision — perhaps it is binding as we agreed on it, but perhaps we'll ignore it and proceed to use the statutory expedited arbitration process when it is in our interest to do so.

(iii) *No strikes — No lock-outs*

The third statutory directive is that every collective agreement must contain a provision that there will be no strikes or lock-outs so long as that collective agreement continues to operate. As in the case of a grievance and arbitration article, if a collective agreement does not contain such a clause or article, either of the parties may request the labour relations board to make an order that the collective agreement shall be deemed to be amended to include such a provision, and thereby fill the negotiating gap. The parties may negotiate language that goes beyond this requirement and, for example, specify the sort of penalties to be invoked in the event that a strike or lock-out takes place. However, as a minimum, there must be an article in every collective agreement that strikes or lock-outs by either party will not take place during the lifetime of the collective agreement. To provide some flesh to this skeletal concept, an example of what is usually called a "No strike — No lock-out" article is as follows:

> **In view of the orderly procedure established by this agreement for the settling of disputes and the handling of grievances, the union agrees that during the lifetime of this agreement there will be no strike, picketing, slow-down or stoppage of work, either complete or partial, and the employer agrees that there will be no lock-out.**

(iv) *Term*

The fourth and final provision that is required by statute in every collective agreement is a termination article. More specifically, there must be an article in every collective agreement which sets out the duration of the collective agreement, in the sense that it establishes an identifiable date on which the collective agreement commences and when it expires. Typically, a termination article will continue by specifying the timing and manner of the giving of notice for the commencement of negotiations for the next collective agreement. The term of a collective agreement may be for as long as the parties agree upon, but the minimum term is one year. Thus, a collective agreement may be in force for a number of years, but it must be in force for at least one year. If this were not the case, effectively, there would be no substantive period during which a collective agreement would operate since the parties would constantly be negotiating the next one. Negotiators, like everyone else, need time to breathe and, sometimes, to heal. By way of illustration, the following language would meet the statutory requirements:

This agreement shall remain in force for a period of two (2) years from the date hereof and shall continue in force from year to year thereafter unless in any year not more than ninety (90) days, and not less than thirty (30) days, before the date of its termination, either party shall furnish the other with notice of termination of, or proposed revision to, this agreement.

(b) Other negotiating subjects

The four subjects discussed above are the only matters that are required by statute to be negotiated. After this it becomes the negotiators' choice. Typically, there are a great many economic and non-economic matters to be addressed at any bargaining table. Many of these topics will be covered in detail at a later stage in this book, but a minimum listing of the subjects for any collective agreement would normally include, in addition to the mandatory provisions, the following:

— Purpose
— Relationship
— Union security
— Management rights
— Stewards
— Seniority
— Wages
— Hours of work and overtime
— Shift differentials
— Vacations with pay
— Paid holidays
— Welfare and benefit provisions
— Job posting

— Bereavement leave
— Jury duty
— Safety and health

The list of subjects for collective bargaining may be as long as the parties wish. There is no obligation for the parties to set out each and every employment benefit, or to cover every employment obligation. However, there may only be one collective agreement in operation at any point in time. Thus, an employer may have a pension plan, but the question of whether that pension plan, together with the pension document that creates the pension obligations, is part of a collective agreement and incorporated in it, depends on the intentions of the parties, what they said, if anything, about pensions in the collective agreement, and whether they negotiated on the pension issue or whether the employer created the plan unilaterally.

There are many instances where a collective agreement will have broad repercussions beyond the immediate work environment and have a significant impact on persons outside a particular collective bargaining relationship. This is generally true of most public sector collective agreements, where tax money collected from citizens forms part or all of the economic resources available to an employer for paying wages and benefits and providing services. It may also be true in the private sector, where an employer is a major force in the economic community or in the industry in which it operates. Similarly, a private sector employer may affect the economic livelihood of suppliers or customers by its own collective bargaining negotiations. For instance, a private sector employer may negotiate a restriction on its right to handle products from suppliers who themselves have collective agreements with a union or group of unions. It is arguable that this form of provision creates liability under the anti-combines legislation, a point which is more a legal caution than a negotiating imperative. The point, however, is that collective bargaining arrangements fashioned by the parties for their own purposes often go beyond the parties to a collective agreement and affect other individuals and parties as well. The effect may be as direct as freezing out a subcontractor if an employer gives up the right to send work outside. Or it may be more indirect by creating a negotiating target or model for one party to use against the other.

Since a collective agreement is between a union on the one hand and an employer on the other, it is only those parties that do the actual negotiating. While there are frequently consultations or other forms of involvement with outside groups or persons, it is the parties to a collective agreement who are subject to the statutory duty to bargain in good faith and to make every reasonable effort to enter into a collective agreement between themselves. There may well be the shadows of other interested parties at the bargaining table if not their actual presence.

Finally, it should be noted that during the time the parties are negotiating for a collective agreement, a union may not lawfully call a strike, and an employer may not lawfully lock out employees who are subject to a collective bargaining relationship, until the conciliation process has been completed and the legal time-clock of the statutory lawful strike provision has run down. In addition, in most jurisdictions an employer is prohibited by law from changing the rates of pay and working conditions of employees without the agreement of the union either from the time the application for certification is received or, in the event of renewal negotiations, from the time notice to bargain is given, until the date when a strike or lock-out may lawfully take place. Thus, while collective bargaining is continuing, until a strike or lock-out would be lawful, the then current wage rates and working conditions are frozen and cannot be changed except by mutual agreement.

The significant point is that negotiations do not begin or end in a vacuum. In part they are shaped and affected by a web of employment laws that must be considered when making negotiating decisions. The impact of pay equity legislation on the issue of wages is but one obvious example. It is not enough to know how to negotiate in the abstract. What is of more value is the knowledge and awareness of what are the significant external and legislative factors that must be considered by a negotiator. What is of greater value still is the acquisition of the skill and the capacity to weave together these separate threads, and to make negotiating sense out of them. What separates the negotiating artist from the novice is the ability to do all of these things, to achieve one's bargaining objectives without the other party feeling it has been exploited.

It is not enough to succeed on the bargaining issues; what is of equal importance is the other side's perception of that success, and whether gaining it has caused the other side to lose face.

Chapter 2

Background to the Bargaining

Collective bargaining is more an art than a science. The objective of the parties is to reach a mutually acceptable collective agreement, but the method by which this is attained is creative and intuitive, at least as much as analytical. Both the intuitive and the analytical roles can be developed with experience. However, while experience is not to be underestimated, the importance of planning and preparation is paramount.

In Canada, there are three separate stages of collective bargaining to be considered: direct bargaining, conciliation, and mediation. This is not to say that each set of negotiations must proceed through all three stages before an agreement is reached. The legal procedure in all provinces is that before a lawful strike or lock-out takes place, the parties must first bargain directly and, if unsuccessful, proceed to conciliation. A conciliation officer must then be appointed, meet with the parties and determine that further conciliation meetings would be of no assistance. Finally, a prescribed time period must elapse after the conciliation officer has left the scene. Only then will the parties be free to engage in lawful economic warfare through the use of a strike or lock-out.

Direct bargaining between parties is precisely what the phrase implies: parties meet and bargain with each other without the involvement of any outside agency and with the purpose of settling their differences by themselves. Whether the collective agreement to be negotiated is a first agreement or a renewal of an existing agreement, the starting point for the parties is to bargain directly with each other before proceeding to the next stage of collective bargaining.

If the parties are bargaining for a first collective agreement, the union begins the process by providing the employer with a formal notice to bargain in accordance with the time periods stipulated in the applicable labour relations Act, usually fifteen days after certification has been granted. In the normal course of events, the union delivers a written notice to bargain — usually a letter — to the employer, states that this constitutes formal notice to bargain, and requests that a mutually acceptable date be set for the commencement of negotiations. If, on the other hand, the collective agreement to be negotiated is a renewal of an existing agreement, notice to bargain would be provided in accordance with the timing and form prescribed in the termination article of the current collective agreement. While it is not always the case, the termination article of a collective agreement will frequently prescribe the point in time before the expiry date of the agreement when either of the parties is free to give notice to the other of its intention to propose amendments for the renewal of the collective agreement. The most common period for the giving of such notice to bargain is either the last ninety days or the last sixty days of a collective agreement. Notice to bargain that is given after the period set out in a collective agreement is still valid, provided it is given before the expiry date of the agreement. If notice is not given, many collective agreements provide for an automatic renewal on the same terms for a one-year period.

If the parties wish, it is quite proper to start bargaining for a new collective agreement on an earlier date than that specified in the termination article. Tactically, it might be felt that this is unwise, since neither party would be under real pressure to reach agreement. If, however, major language revisions are involved and the bargaining sincerity of both of the parties is genuine, the extra time and the absence of a strike mentality may be just what is needed. If the parties are trying to avoid a future confrontation and want to rewrite a collective agreement that is confusing and has caused disputes between them, negotiations held before an agreement's expiry date may be more productive and less emotional than negotiations held when the clock is running down and the strike potential is building up. Obviously, both parties must approach such negotiation meetings with the intention to make necessary changes in language, and must be willing to compromise; otherwise the meetings will not produce results. Solutions to bargaining disputes are not generated in the air; they are created by negotiators who can first identify a problem, and then find a solution both sides can accept.

If agreement is reached through early negotiations and the new terms are to take effect before the old collective agreement has expired, the law is clear that the new provisions cannot be implemented, nor can a new agreement replace an existing agreement, without the consent of the appropriate labour relations board. The purpose of this requirement is to avoid private deals between an employer and a union that are intended to block a second union from raiding the first union and obtaining bargaining rights, or to prevent employees from terminating the bargaining rights of the first union because a new agreement has been imposed upon them before the old one expired.

1. First Collective Agreement — Union Role

Let us assume notice to bargain has been given by a union that has been granted certification as the bargaining agent of a given group of employees. The certification trauma is over and the parties must prepare for negotiations. The parties must focus on their strategic goals and objectives, as well as the tone and substance of their new relationship.

The first order of business, from the union perspective, is the selection of a bargaining committee from among the employees in the bargaining unit. An employee or agent of the union itself will be appointed as the person to lead the bargaining committee in conducting the actual negotiations and, quite possibly, to act as the spokesperson. Once the bargaining committee has been established, it must prepare draft proposals. The vocabulary of bargaining is always interesting. The person who makes the initial requests will use the term "proposals". The person who receives these proposals will rename them "demands".

There is no uniformity in the way unions prepare proposals for a first collective agreement. In most instances, membership meetings are convened for the bargaining committee and the employees to discuss their particular problems and concerns; these discussions may in turn be incorporated into collective agreement proposals. In addition, the union representative may make recommendations to the other members of the bargaining committee, and an expression of opinion from the membership may be required. In essence, the union consults its membership to identify important issues. The task of fashioning language and formal collective agreement wording is then left to the bargaining committee.

The formulation of proposals for a first collective agreement is a difficult task for any union bargaining committee. The employees who are selected from the membership and placed on the bargaining committee are likely to be inexperienced and unsophisticated in collective bargaining matters. The employees' expectations may have risen to an unrealistic degree during the organizing campaign that led to the certification order, and the employees may want immediate and dramatic action. In addition, people usually join a union because they feel they need its services to remedy problems in their workplace; this need, real or perceived, may emanate from management errors, which will in turn be a focal point of the bargaining proposals. Simply put, employees may want specific action on the matters or issues at their place of work that gave rise to their interest in the union in the first place.

Some of the matters troubling the membership may be serious and substantial, but collective bargaining may not provide them with the answers. For instance, some industrial operations, such as foundries, are hot, dirty and noisy. While some physical and engineering steps may be taken to relieve a measure of the discomfort, the nature of an operation cannot be changed by the language of a collective agreement. On the other hand, some pragmatic steps may help: one could identify the range of physical discomfort and propose economic sanctions such as "dirty work" premiums, extra break periods, and so on, in an effort to make a task more palatable. If a task itself cannot be changed, the effects on employees can be recognized and, in part, compensated for by arranging for the task to be performed for a shorter period of time, or by paying additional money, or both.

The preparation of proposals is also influenced by activities or unfair labour practices that took place while a certification application was underway. Events during the organizing campaign may have created tension and frustration between employees and their employer. As has been stated, the granting of a certification order by the appropriate labour relations board depends on the statutory requirements of that board as to the percentage of employees who must be members of the applicant union when a certification application is filed. In most jurisdictions, provision is made in the Act or in the regulations for those employees who do not wish the applicant union to represent them to intervene in the certification procedures, and to oppose an application through a petition or other form of presentation. In many cases, charges of unfair labour practices result from such employee interventions, which in turn lead to acrimonious disputes and hearings. Labour relations, like physics, has its own laws of action and counteraction. Indeed, in some applications, both parties end up accusing each other, at each stage of the proceedings, of unlawful conduct, followed by denials, refutations and countercharges. Regardless of the outcome of an intervention or the result of any charges, this legal alley-fight is bound to cause hard feelings among the employer, the union and at least some employees, especially those who have been directly involved as representatives or witnesses in the hearings.

While it is a generalization, it can be said that the more heated a certification proceeding, the more difficult it will be for both an employer negotiating team and a union bargaining committee to approach a bargaining table without a high degree of emotionalism. The judgment of both parties will be coloured by the effect of the hearing of any charges of unfair labour practices, and the blood-letting that is common to such proceedings. It is unrealistic to expect that parties who have gone through a bitter series of exchanges, during what may have been days of hearings before a certification order was issued, can wipe from their minds the anger that was generated, and sit down to bargain together in a calm, rational manner. It has been the author's experience that the most heated first collective agreement negotiations are a result of antagonistic certification proceedings, with the usual panoply of petitions, charges and countercharges which sometimes result from the desperate steps taken to avoid automatic certification, that is, certification without a representation vote by employees in the bargaining unit. In this respect our legislators could learn from the American experience where certification is not granted without a representation vote, with a resulting improvement in the Canadian collective bargaining climate.

It is in the context of a particular certification proceeding that the union representative must decide what to put in the initial collective agreement proposal. This is especially so if the organizing campaign was based upon a commitment to obtain parity with some other employer's wages or working conditions. If the campaign was based upon a generalized promise of "more", specific items and targets must be agreed upon to form part of any first collective agreement proposals. If, during an organizing campaign, union members have been led to believe that certification and the bargaining muscle of the union will bring about dramatic changes in their employment conditions and benefits through collective bargaining, those general expectations will have to be translated into detailed and specific initial proposals.

A union representative may be in a dilemma in advising employees as to what their collective agreement proposals should be. The employees may be united and aggressively determined to attain certain collective bargaining results. The union representative may conclude, nevertheless, that such objectives are unrealistic and, in the bargaining circumstances, unreasonable. The union representative, in most cases, would have the experience to know that any collective agreement requires a mutual compromise of interests that are often competing, if only from a political point of view. In the result, the union representative must consider whether the initial collective agreement proposals being discussed by the membership are so extreme or inflammatory as to cause the employer to be totally negative, not only to the specific proposals, but to the very idea of entering into any collective agreement with a union that is making such outrageous demands.

Expressed another way, a union is entitled to ask for anything it wishes in its proposals, but it must recognize that the proposals are of no real value to the membership unless and until the employer is persuaded to agree to some or all of them. If the initial proposals are indefensible and likely to cause the employer to reject them out of hand, a responsible union representative should consider advising the members to modify their proposals before they are tabled with the employer.

The difficulty here is that the union representative is, and must be seen to be, the employees' spokesperson, with a responsibility to represent them and to achieve, in whole or in part, their bargaining objectives. In many cases the employees on the bargaining committee are in a contradictory position: on the one hand they are representatives of their fellow employees; on the other hand they have their own concerns and expectations. Not surprisingly, their bargaining perspective is limited to the particular operation where they work. The union representative, on the other hand, should have the ability to judge whether a given proposal is realistic in the light of the current bargaining climate. The real question is whether the union representative wants to be the leader or the captive of the employees.

One practical way in which the union representative may balance responsibility and potential reality is to ensure that the union proposals, especially in the economic area, are unspecific and open-ended. For instance, rather than specify a wage proposal of a precise amount that then becomes a fixed target in the employees' minds, a vague and deliberately fuzzy phrase such as "substantial wage increase" can be employed to create some strategic fog behind which a negotiator can manoeuvre. Thus, the union representative can satisfy the militants, and yet not become locked into wage proposals that cannot be pressed seriously.

Practically speaking, the union bargaining committee must develop proposals for both the economic areas of a collective agreement and the administrative or non-economic areas. Its task is to draft, in full and flowing detail, a complete collective agreement that incorporates the collective bargaining aspirations of the employees, to present to the employer at the first formal bargaining meeting. Thus, the union bargaining committee must not only make decisions as to the principles it wants embodied in a collective agreement, but also draft language which sets out the precise formulation of those principles, and how they are to be applied and administered. For instance, the union bargaining committee would be expected to determine the form of union security that it wants, and to draft a proposed article to reflect that decision, together with the details of how and when union dues are to be deducted from employees, when they are to be forwarded to the union, to whom, and so on. Similarly, language would be drafted for or by the union bargaining committee which would set out the form of seniority article to be sought, and would also define what is meant by seniority, how it accumulates, when it is lost, what weight is to be given to it, and under what circumstances — in short, a road-map in words to show how seniority will apply in that particular workplace.

Many unions have research departments or facilities which are of assistance to the union representative and the bargaining committee in providing information and recommendations for them to evaluate in relation to their collective agreement proposals. Most unions have spent time and energy in preparing models of every conceivable collective bargaining clause that ingenious minds can conceive. In addition, many have available a wealth of statistical and comparative data on all bargaining issues. To that extent the union bargaining committee is often far better informed and armed, in a statistical sense, than its employer counterpart.

In evaluating the best way to use this comparative material, the union bargaining committee bears two objectives in mind. First, the information should be examined to help the union bargaining committee to decide on the substance and content of the collective agreement proposals, and what is the available range of contractual options. This examination helps identify those provisions in other collective agreements that can be used as appropriate models, either as part of the initial proposals or as backups as negotiating events unfold. Apart from this, another objective is served. Obviously, at the very best, it can be expected that each of the bargaining proposals will be the subject of debate and argument by the employer negotiating team, and the union will want to be able to mount a rational defence of each proposal, by the use of comparative information, when the employer's attack begins. On the other hand, if no such information exists, now is the best time to learn this fact, before an indefensible bargaining position is taken.

In summary, the members of the union bargaining committee must be appointed and collective agreement proposals drafted in consultation with the membership and the union representative. The collective agreement proposals should be weighed not only in the abstract sense of being desirable because of their particular merit, but also from the point of view of whether there are realistic grounds to think they can be achieved at the bargaining table. One way to answer that question is to examine what other collective agreements between employers in the same or a comparable industry or sector provide, to determine the options and potential supporting arguments available when the negotiators come to grips — literally and metaphorically — with that issue.

2. First Collective Agreement — Employer Role

From an employer's point of view, the period before the commencement of the bargaining meetings is a time of self-recrimination, because of the union presence and any nervousness about the bargaining. It is also a period during which the employer should be preparing and organizing for bargaining, in both a strategic and conceptual sense. An analogy can be made to gardening. If the flowerbeds are not first located, then dug, sown and watered, the seeds will not grow. The time for doing the preparation work is now, before the bargaining begins.

Just as the union members will have made decisions as to who will be bargaining on behalf of their bargaining unit, an employer must select its own negotiating team. An employer negotiating team should be chosen for a specific purpose, in the sense that each member of that team will have a defined role that will assist and advance the negotiations. On the union side, a bargaining committee will likely consist of an outside union representative and several employees appointed or elected by the union members of the bargaining unit. An employer is free to select any person it wishes to conduct negotiations on its behalf; a union has no right in law to dictate who will take part in the actual bargaining on behalf of an employer. By the same token, a bargaining unit appoints its own bargaining committee and the employer cannot object to any individual member being present at negotiations. An employer may retain the services of an outside consultant, including a lawyer, in the same manner as a union bargaining committee may utilize the knowledge and bargaining expertise of a business agent or union representative.

There is no great value in having a large number of persons on either an employer negotiating team or a union bargaining committee. To the contrary, the larger a team or committee, the more unwieldy the negotiations may become, if only because every individual may feel under an obligation to take an active role in the bargaining. What is important is quality, not quantity. Some union bargaining committees are structured to provide representation from the different employee groups in an operation. This arrangement enables each member of a union bargaining committee to speak to those issues that affect the particular group represented by that member.

It is difficult to be precise as to the size and composition of an employer negotiating team. The author's experience is that there should be included one or more persons who have direct and personal knowledge of the employer's employment and industrial relations policies, as well as how the employer's business is conducted in an operational sense. Both operations and personnel must be represented on the employer negotiating team, as each is equally affected and impacted by any bargaining decisions. Both are vital stakeholders.

It is generally inadvisable for the senior executive officer of an employer to be at the bargaining table, certainly not on a regular basis. There are several reasons for this. In the first place, the collective bargaining process is likely to be lengthy, and it may be assumed that the time of a senior executive officer is more profitably spent in making policy and operating decisions. In the second place, if during bargaining questions are asked of a senior executive officer, or a commitment is sought, it becomes difficult to avoid giving an immediate response, when in fact calling time out would be more beneficial either to cool things down or to gain time for reflection and analysis. In the third place, the absence of a senior executive officer enables the employer negotiating team to get appropriate instructions, particularly when important negotiating decisions are being made. Obviously, a union bargaining committee is obligated to report to its principals, namely the bargaining unit members, and an employer negotiating team has a corresponding responsibility to the senior executive officer or officers in the organization and the board of directors. These reports should be made away from the bargaining table for the purpose of receiving direction and guidance, rather than in a direct participatory role.

Apart from these considerations, the members of the employer negotiating team should also be selected for the specific knowledge they have and the information they can contribute. For example, if an industrial plant is the employer, there should be someone on the negotiating team who has detailed knowledge of the plant operations, at least to the extent of knowing how any change in such operations would affect employees. At the same time there should also be a member of the negotiating team, such as a controller, who can speak to the economic issues that are raised and discussed during bargaining, and who has the capacity to calculate the costings as required. Further, a negotiating team should have a member with knowledge or experience in the drafting of collective bargaining language and skill with words, both oral and written, as well as an understanding of the collective bargaining process as a whole. The facility to draft language with clarity, precision and, on occasion, speed is a great advantage to any negotiator. Unfortunately, an ability to express complex concepts in clear and simple words is as rare as common sense, but experience does help.

3. Bargaining Roles

The employer negotiating team must agree on the bargaining rules and the role each team member will play at the bargaining meetings. One of the members should be designated as the spokesperson for the team. Ground rules as to how the negotiating team will function must be established, so that the negotiators do operate as a team, and do not trip over their own negotiating feet.

What kind of rules are we talking about? Experienced members of union bargaining committees and employer negotiating teams have their own sets of cues and signals to let their fellow members know when caucus is needed, or that the person talking is getting into dangerous negotiating waters. Similarly, they should agree in advance whether all the talking at the bargaining table is to be done by a spokesperson, how direct questions addressed to others are to be answered, and by whom.

No magic formula exists, but as a rule the fewer the people who speak at the bargaining table the less likely it is there will be conflict and contradiction. In addition, negotiating has its own vocabulary and code words, and the wrong message can easily be given inadvertently. Not only should a negotiating team or bargaining committee function smoothly, but also, more importantly, it should be seen by the other side to operate with co-ordination. This can only happen if communications and roles are assigned, planned and understood.

A story may illustrate what happens if this is not done. Early in my negotiating career I was involved in a difficult and strained negotiating meeting. Positions were hardening, tempers were flaring, and the emotional heat was rising. Without consulting with my own group, I decided to cool things off by having a caucus. I waited until there was a suitable break, stood up, and looking appropriately serious, headed for the door. My fellow members, who had not been briefed, looked up in confusion. I stood and looked at them, and they stared back. The drama of the move was disappearing. Finally, one of my group asked, "Where in hell are you going? The bar isn't open yet!"

Before we discuss the subject of how and where to do research for negotiations, some comment should be made about the location of negotiating meetings. The question may arise as to whether negotiating meetings should take place on the employer's premises or at some neutral location such as a hotel meeting room. The usual practice is that both parties want such meetings to be held away from a plant or other operation, on neutral ground. If the meetings are on the employer's premises, undoubtedly interruptions will take place and there will be a break in the concentration of all concerned. Practically speaking, it is difficult for the members of either group to avoid being pinned down by other employees during breaks or other intervals when the negotiations are taking place at the workplace. A further difficulty is that there may be no suitable place where either or both parties may consult in private — an important element of any negotiating meeting.

The only difficulty with an outside location is the cost of the facilities. Of course, the parties may make any cost-sharing arrangement they wish, but it is such a minimal element in the scheme of things that most parties simply rotate the cost of the meeting room, or the employer pays for the meeting room and the union, if it wishes, provides its own caucus room.

Another factor that may be troublesome is whether an employer is obliged by law to pay the wages of employee members of a union bargaining committee for the time spent in negotiations. In the absence of a provision existing in a particular collective agreement, no such legal obligation exists. Many employers understandably bridle at being asked to pay wages to persons who are negotiating against them, even when such persons are their own employees. Some idealists decry the fact that the negotiating process is adversarial, and hope for a greater unity of purpose and a more generous attitude. Nonetheless, the parties are adversaries, in the sense that one party wants more of what the other party has or controls, and it is asking too much of human nature to expect an employer not to think of the employees on a union bargaining committee as being on the opposite side. In fact, since collective bargaining is simply the resolution through discussion of competing interests, pretending the process is not adversarial is at best hypocritical and at worst destructive, in that it removes both the need and the means for reaching agreement, and the problem, like unpaid taxes, compounds itself.

Some unions are also opposed to the idea of a union bargaining committee member's wages being paid by an employer; they take the position that during the time spent in the actual bargaining, the members of a union bargaining committee should feel no sense of commitment or obligation to their employer. As a result, many unions arrange to pay their own bargaining committee members for the time they are off work due to bargaining. While there is nothing to prevent an employer from agreeing to pay wages to employees who are on a union bargaining committee, such an arrangement is more common where an employer and a union have a long-standing collective agreement relationship, and emotional attitudes concerning the role of the union have stabilized. Even then, the arrangement the parties reach will often cover negotiations up to, but not including, the conciliation process. In other words, the employees will be paid by the employer only during the direct bargaining between the parties. After that point the wages will be the responsibility of the union. This makes some logical sense in view of the fact that conciliation is much more frequently invoked by unions than by employers. If a union chooses to escalate the process and to turn the bargaining screws, the employer may respond by expecting the union to bear at least this part of the cost.

Chapter 3

Preparation for Negotiations

A collective agreement does not arrive unannounced. It is the product of much effort and energy applied to planning and preparation. The resulting agreement is a direct reflection of the quality of preparation.

The time to start preparing for negotiations on the next collective agreement is during the term of the existing collective agreement. Obviously, certain provisions of an existing collective agreement may create difficulties in application or interpretation for both the employer and the union. A clause may have been badly drafted and, therefore, be difficult to interpret or apply in day-to-day situations. Similarly, an article may cause unexpected or unforeseen results in certain fact situations that were not contemplated or considered by the negotiators. In such circumstances, the parties to the negotiations should make a record of these language problems as they arise. The historical record is probably the best indicator of how well a collective agreement is working in practice.

Wise employers, as a matter of regular routine, instruct supervisors to keep a running record of all problems created by the particular language of the collective agreement that a supervisor is required to administer. One simple method is to hand out copies of the current collective agreement with a blank page between each printed page so that notations may be made by a supervisor as events occur. A note may be as specific as a supervisor wishes, but should give enough useful detail to serve as a memory jogger when the supervisors are next jointly reviewing the collective agreement. The obvious fact is that supervisors are more likely to know the operating flaws or failings in any collective agreement, since they have to make operating decisions, based on their reading of the language in the agreement, on a daily basis. Thus, their opinions on necessary revisions to a collective agreement are important, in that they know, or should know, what has and has not worked in the agreement.

On the union side, the same technique is often followed. Any member of a union may keep a record, but more commonly this is done by stewards or bargaining committee members. Again, the purpose is to leave a paper trail of incidents where language difficulties with an existing collective agreement have arisen. In short, both employer and union negotiators will benefit from an examination of the records, before the start of negotiations, on those parts of an existing collective agreement that are in need of revision, as well as the reasons for those revisions and any thoughts about proposed changes that would remedy a problem.

An equally important resource tool is an examination of a list of grievances and complaints presented during the lifetime of the current collective agreement. Grievances that have arisen, particularly where they are repetitive, serve to identify current collective agreement language that is causing difficulties. If a grievance has been taken to arbitration, the analysis and interpretation of a collective agreement provision in the arbitrator's decision is of great significance to the parties in deciding whether a change in the current wording is needed, or precisely how a clause should be reworded. If the grievance in question revolves around a factual situation, as is the case, for example, with most discharge or discipline disputes, the arbitrator's decision may be of marginal value in determining a need for changes to the collective agreement wording. On the other hand, if a grievance appears to have resulted from confusion or uncertainty as to the meaning of an article, there may be a need to do something about the language used in the collective agreement in order to avoid a continuation of the dispute that brought about the grievance.

1. Comparative Agreements

Collective agreements are not negotiated in a vacuum of information and comparative data. The negotiations are shaped, to some degree, by comparisons prepared by both parties of other collective agreements in the same industry or in the particular community or region. What another employer and union have said and done in another collective agreement will have a direct impact as a reference point, if not a negotiating target, especially if the other employer is in a related sector or industry or if the same union is involved. In some cases, industrial or area patterns of parallel or identical settlements, where they can be objectively compiled from an examination of uniform rates or conditions of employment in the same or a similar business, may dictate the results of the negotiations if the parties agree on what the pattern is, and accept its logic. In any event, if a pattern can be identified as the result of an analysis of other agreements, it can be used as an indicator to negotiators as to what their settlement should be. Each negotiating party must assume the other side will try to find the dimensions of that pattern, so it can be used offensively as a negotiating justification, or defensively as a negotiating ambush. If either party intends to use comparative information, it must first find the information, and then see how it can best be used. If one of the parties intends to contest the existence or the significance of any comparative pattern, that party must understand the substance of the information in order to develop a counter-strategy. Either way, the information must be obtained, collated and then analyzed for its value and application to the circumstances.

For these reasons, each party will want to find as much specific information as it can, and obtain copies of any collective agreements that might be relevant to its own negotiations. Many unions have a sophisticated and extensive research branch, which produces this information for union negotiators whenever they need it. Many employer negotiators fail to appreciate the value of such information, or do not want to spend the time and effort required to figure out how to use it. In addition, some employers are reluctant to share with other employers information about their collective agreements, with the result that employer interests generally suffer from an overdose of labour relations secrecy. Recently, more employers have begun to exchange information about their collective agreements on a regular basis. This may help to change the image of some employers as badly informed and narrow in their negotiating perspective. Whether the information is going to be used at all, or precisely how, is beside the point at this stage. Information, like wine, can't be used unless you've got it when you want it.

The negotiators should identify and obtain copies of the particular collective agreements they wish to evaluate well before negotiations are due to begin. These collective agreements should be carefully analyzed to assess whether the respective articles apply to the negotiating employer's operating situation. If an article is of little or no application, there is no point in being concerned with the merits of the wording. If an article does apply, it should be studied to see whether the language is more favourable than the wording in the current collective agreement, and, if so, precisely why that is the case and what words accomplish this result. From the employer's side, an article should be examined to determine whether it is providing a condition or benefit greater or lesser than that provided in the existing collective agreement. At the same time, the provision should be assessed for clarity of language and compared with the existing article to weigh its effectiveness in accomplishing the employer's aim. From the union point of view, a careful examination of an article will determine whether it can be used as justification for a demand for change and improvement in the forthcoming negotiations. Even more importantly, it can give the negotiators a model, a negotiating option, or a specific target to focus on. It also means that one is dealing with hard facts that may be used as a tool, rather than with uninformed expectations. Lastly, the negotiator will begin to appreciate the strengths and weaknesses of the other side's negotiating arguments.

Other collective agreements, together with available statistics, should be used to review the wage and benefit patterns in the particular industry, community or geographic area. Before going into negotiations, both parties should assess the relationship between the wages and benefits provided by the employer and those of the employer's competitors in the community. In making such comparisons, the greater the similarities in operations, specific jobs and geography, the better. At the same time, general economic information should be reviewed, such as the latest cost-of-living figures, changes in interest rates and other costs of doing business, so as to provide a broader perspective and context. Again, a negotiator needs this data not only to shape and frame proposals, but also to respond to and attack positions from the other side.

Let me throw a bit of cold water on the enthusiastic endorsement of the use of information. While compiling comparative data is valuable and necessary, it is not a magic wand. A comparison should be made coldly and objectively in the light of the real facts, not the facts as you would like them to be. It is of little value for a negotiator to put together a number of tables or calculations which are not comparisons of the same things. For instance, in wage comparisons, base rates should not be compared with job rates. If jobs are to be compared, they should be compared with identical or similar jobs, not with dissimilar jobs. Job titles may be the same in two different collective agreements, but the content of the actual jobs may be quite unalike; this distinction may justify a disparity between the two rates. The wage rates may be almost identical, but the hours of work of two different operations may not be; this fact will affect the validity of a comparison based on rates alone. One employer may pay similar or even identical wages, but provide very different employment benefits, which again will distort a comparison. The point is that an examination should be done with care, and directed at a determination of all the facts. At a superficial level, the facts may seem clear, but it is necessary to go behind the wording of similar wage schedules, for instance, to get at the respective job duties, to be sure that apples are being compared with apples and not prunes.

2. Strategy

Strategy is as important to collective bargaining as it is to achieving political office. Simply put, a bargaining strategy is an action plan — the way in which you want to reach your objective.

Each party, when preparing to bargain on its next collective agreement, should work on its respective overall plan or strategy long before the parties actually meet. Since the aim of any negotiations is to reach a mutually satisfactory agreement, the strategy of both sides should be a road-map of how and where the parties can meet.

Perhaps the most important single component in devising a bargaining strategy, regardless of whether one is on the union or employer side, is the element of timing, or the expected date of reaching agreement. Timing is all-important. It is critical at two levels. First, a proposal put forward before a party is ready to accept, or at least conditioned to receive it, will likely be rejected, not because the proposal has no merit but because the timing is wrong. Secondly, the timing of the negotiating process must be thought through; each move must fit the strategic purpose of either quickening the negotiating pace or slowing it down. Thus, there are specific timing issues, such as when to move or to counter, and general timing issues, such as, is it likely a collective agreement can be reached before the summer holidays, and if not, what are the consequences?

An issue that requires a fine judgment is whether the negotiations should be pushed to an early conclusion or, in contrast, whether either or both parties see any advantage in dragging their negotiating feet and playing for time, by ensuring the parties become involved in other stages of negotiation such as conciliation or mediation. One gains time because a strike cannot take place until conciliation is completed. To answer this question requires an analysis of a party's own negotiating strengths and weaknesses, as well as an objective consideration of the position of the other side. The union strategists, for instance, would have to examine the mood and temper of the majority of employees in the bargaining unit. What are their expectations for gains in a new collective agreement, and how determined are they to attain these objectives? What financial resources are available to the local union in the event of a strike? What is the current public view of strikes? What outside support, if any, can be expected from other unionists or interested groups who may see the issues as worth supporting?

From an employer perspective, the same questions would be asked. What is the employer's assessment of the attitude of the employees? Are they militant and, if so, over what issues? What is the inventory position? What are the completion dates for existing orders? How vulnerable is the employer to pressure from suppliers and customers? Can a product boycott hurt? And so on.

Collective bargaining negotiations can be as brief or as prolonged as one or both parties wish. It is unusual for both parties to have the same priorities and negotiating strategies, at least on the question of timing. Each of the parties decides on its own timetable, in the sense of what will best serve its negotiating purposes, and what events it can reasonably be expected to control in accordance with the timing schedule, despite what the other party may say or do. This requires the party making a particular strategy decision not only to understand and appreciate its own strengths and weaknesses, but to go further and question whether it is able to seize and maintain control of the negotiations, or whether the other side, by reason of superior negotiating strength, can itself dictate the pace of bargaining in relation to its agenda.

While a determination of the appropriate negotiating strategy is primarily prospective — that is, deciding what combination of concepts and timing will work in the future — one valuable resource tool is to review the past negotiating patterns of the same parties. If the past bargaining analysis discloses both a pattern and a resulting strike or other form of confrontation, perhaps a change in the bargaining strategy this time around is required. If the former negotiations went smoothly, and particularly if the same strategy has been followed for a number of sets of negotiations, there may be little value in adopting a new or different approach. Put another way, the parties may have established a collective bargaining pattern which may be virtually impossible to break, because they have always negotiated in that manner and all the participants will expect the same pattern to be followed this time. A bargaining machine may work well or not at all. But, if everyone knows its foibles, why fix it!

For example, if past negotiations have usually resulted in meetings that are a waste of time and energy until conciliation has been exhausted and a strike deadline set, it will be difficult to reverse the pattern and expect the parties to engage in serious and meaningful bargaining at the first meeting. Why? Because negotiators are very suspicious of a change in a bargaining pattern, especially when the other side wants the change and where such change will demonstrably benefit only that party. As a result, if you want to create a new pattern, think how you can best persuade the other side to go along, or you will end up bargaining with yourself.

With respect to preparing for negotiations, one further point should be made. Many collective bargaining issues are not generated in a vacuum, but result from real or perceived operating disputes in a particular workplace. The dispute may not involve a direct violation of an existing collective agreement. The genesis may be only in the manner or method by which an order was given to an employee, but that employee's emotional response or reaction may be so dramatic as to escalate the misunderstanding into a major dispute. Again, the questionable judgment of a supervisor may be so blatant that some employees become convinced that favouritism or discrimination is present in job posting decisions, or in determining merit increases for individual employees. It may be the case that nothing can be accomplished by filing a grievance under the current collective agreement, yet the heat and the passion is palpable. A union can and must react by correcting an injustice through changes to a seniority article generally, and a job posting provision in particular, or, in the example of a seniority article or an alleged discrimination in a wage area, by attacking the very concept of merit increases.

It is not enough to decide as you prepare for negotiations what you want to achieve. What about the other side? What is troubling it, and why? How is it likely to react to your concern? Where, you ask, is it coming from? Thus, it is in the interests of both parties to consider the views and attitudes of each other on the application and administration of an existing collective agreement, in order to gauge what is likely to be tabled as a collective bargaining demand by the other party. If this is done, the other side can at least consider whether steps can be taken to defuse an issue before collective bargaining begins. If there is an obvious operating irritant, can it be removed now, before it causes more bargaining trouble than it is worth? If not, would a meeting with the affected employees to explain more fully the purpose of the operating procedure reduce some of the tension? Is it useful, in a tactical sense, to maintain a position now, then use its removal as a bargaining chip, and get something in return?

3. Labour-Management Committees

Having enough objective information to properly form these judgments is one of the major results where the parties to a collective agreement have some form of ongoing mechanism so that the two sides maintain contact and have discussions on matters of mutual interest during the life of an agreement. The most common means to accomplish this purpose is a labour-management committee, which meets periodically, or as required, outside of both the collective bargaining negotiations and the deliberations of a grievance committee. The purpose of such meetings is not to discuss grievances, or to act as a grievance committee, but to examine in a general way in-plant problems that are causing one or both sides some difficulty. It cannot be said too often that collective bargaining issues are frequently a reflection of frustrations arising out of the day-to-day application of an existing collective agreement. A problem begins as an operating decision and ends as a bargaining demand. A concern may be justified, or it may be caused not by inadequacies in the language of a collective agreement, but by the quality of, or more accurately the lack of quality in, an individual supervisor's decision, which seems to be unfair or unreasonable to some employees. If an employer, as part of its in-house management of labour relations, provides no opportunity to employees and their representatives to vent their feelings and express their concerns, it is inevitable that these will be aired at the bargaining table. When that happens it may be more difficult to resolve any problems, without substantive language changes, in the heightened emotions and more formal atmosphere of the bargaining process.

As a result, some form of labour-management discussions, operating entirely apart from the formal grievance procedure, can serve to release any emotional steam that may exist, and provide a more restrained and unpressured opportunity to address any problems. Nor should this kind of forum be viewed as a negative thing. Some employers have learned much useful information at such meetings, and have cemented some solid relationships, by responding constructively to criticism that was merited and by involving union representatives in the search for a solution. It is difficult to work together effectively if you never talk together or try to communicate.

4. Amendments to Agreements

Every collective agreement must be for a term certain, in that it has a date on which it comes into effect and a date on which it expires. In most jurisdictions, the term of a collective agreement must be for a minimum period of one year. Apart from this restriction, the parties may choose to enter into a collective agreement for whatever longer period of time they wish, whether it be two, three or more years. While a collective agreement continues in full force and effect during the entire period of its operation, the parties may, if they choose, agree on changes or amendments to the agreement at any time, and on whatever terms they wish. The exception is that they may not agree to change the article which sets out the date the collective agreement terminates, and establish a new expiry date, without obtaining the consent of the appropriate labour relations board to the early termination of the old collective agreement. To be clear, the consent is not to the fact of negotiating a new termination date, but to the consequence of such change. A new expiry date is not effective until the board has given its consent.

If the parties decide that an existing article is not working effectively because the language is badly drafted, they may have meetings to discuss the article. If they decide on new and better language, by changing, adding or deleting words, they can agree to a formal amendment of an existing article to conform with the understanding they have reached. Any agreement to amend a collective agreement must be in writing, and the document setting out such amending agreement should clearly state whether the new language is to replace an existing article. It should also state the actual date when the newly amended language comes into effect. A document that sets out an amendment need not be complicated or formalistic; a simple letter will be sufficient, provided it is clear as to what the parties have agreed on and is signed by both parties.

As a general rule, a collective agreement should not be subjected to repeated changes and amendments during its lifetime. If a party insists on a wording change, or an amendment, to correct any deficiency each time it experiences some difficulty with a provision of the collective agreement, the net effect will be constant negotiation of the collective agreement. This lack of contractual stability would be most unsatisfactory, since neither of the parties would have any certainty with regard to its own rights and obligations under the collective agreement, and the process of mutual trade-offs that brought about the agreement in the first place would be undercut. This is particularly so with respect to additions to a collective agreement, in contrast to revisions made to an existing article. As to the former, that is, an accretion or addition of new or different benefits or rights, the invariable practice of both union and employer is to refuse to make contractual additions while an existing collective agreement is in operation. With respect to revisions to existing language, it is not possible to be as definitive as to the wisdom of making changes. Certainly, it is fundamental that the parties should accept responsibility for any consequences arising out of the language of a collective agreement they negotiated, for better or for worse. On the other hand, the seriousness of a problem may be mounting. As a consequence, it may be in the parties' respective interests to negotiate an amendment to the collective agreement rather than wait for the commencement of negotiations for a new agreement. This is particularly so if the current agreement has an extended period of time before it expires.

Some collective agreements were first negotiated a good many years ago and have been added to on a piecemeal basis, to the extent that the parties are faced with convoluted and, in some cases, contradictory language throughout an agreement. If this is the situation, the parties may wish to revise the language extensively, not so much for the purpose of changing the intent of an offending article, but to define more clearly for themselves what an article means and how it is to be applied. In such a case, the parties might be wise to enter into discussions before formal negotiations for a new collective agreement have commenced. At least in theory, it can be hoped that the parties will not then be under time pressures that might deflect their attention, and the atmosphere between them will be more relaxed and easy.

Chapter 4

Principles of Negotiations

The object of negotiations is to reach a mutually acceptable agreement. This is equally the case whether the subject of negotiations is a collective agreement or some other form of agreement such as a contract for the sale or purchase of an automobile. Negotiating can be contrasted with debating. Negotiating involves the fashioning of compromises to accommodate the competing interests and concerns of the parties. Debating, on the other hand, is its antithesis. Debating is the opposite of compromise, namely, the victory of one party over another or, as a necessary corollary, the defeat of one party. To put the matter more graphically, debating causes someone to lose and, as a consequence, gives rise to a scoreboard mentality. In contrast, negotiating involves deliberate and purposeful accommodation to ensure that the other party does not appear to lose, and to gain credits that can be profitably used as the negotiations unfold.

Negotiating is an exercise in problem solving, but the problem in question is not a problem for one party alone. Since both parties must find a way to resolve it together, a problem for one party is necessarily a problem for the other. The way this problem solving exercise unfolds can be broken down into three components — identification, evaluation and resolution — each of which will now be analyzed.

1. Identification

A problem must be identified not only in the generic sense — that is, by finding an appropriate label that can be applied to it, such as wages — but the precise parameters of a problem must also be examined so that its full dimensions are known. In addition, there must be some mutual examination of the problem itself and the negotiation terrain that surrounds it. It is for that reason that experienced negotiators spend a good deal of time talking about a given issue. Their purpose is to ensure that they fully understand the problem and all of its facets. They do this first, because they recognize that solving a problem requires first that one understand it.

There is another reason for doing the analysis in this order. If a problem is to be mutually resolved, and if understanding is a precondition to resolution, it follows that both parties must understand it together. Clearly, both parties will be coming at a problem from different directions. Typically, one party is seeking a particular change or benefit, and the other party is saying "No!". The importance of identification is not with respect to the response. In most cases, this is self-evident, but in a sense it is peripheral. What is significant is an understanding of the change itself, the language that is proposed to implement such change, how that change would apply in particular circumstances, and what the operating consequences would be if it were incorporated into the collective agreement.

2. Evaluation

Let us assume that the negotiating parties are stuck on a union demand for a job posting provision to be added to the existing seniority language of the current collective agreement. The negotiators have identified the dimensions of the problem, in that they have reviewed at length the problem the change is intended to solve, the language proposed, how it would work, to whom it would apply, and all of the operating characteristics of the demand. Now their concern is with evaluating the demand.

Any given demand must be evaluated in two contexts. The first is the reason for the demand. In the above example, this requires an examination of the past practices of the operation in dealing with promotions and the awarding of jobs. Has there been any system of job preference? Has there been any way in which an individual employee could let the employer know that he or she had a particular interest in a job when there has been an opening? Was there any co-ordination in making promotions, or were individuals who had become supervisors left to their own judgment? Is this the first time the matter has been raised in negotiations? Has the union been able to bring forward any specific examples of real or perceived injustice or discrimination? If so, is there any truth to these allegations?

The second context is in terms of the future. The question to ask is "How will the provision affect the operation?" This, in turn, leads to a number of different issues. How often do job opportunities become available? Bearing in mind the normal rate of turnover, how many jobs can one reasonably expect to fill during the lifetime of a collective agreement? Is the workforce likely to expand, and if so, will this open up job opportunities? Is the business such that most of the existing employees can, with very little training, move into whatever jobs become available, or are specialized skills required that may compel the employer to go outside the workforce to fill vacancies? These questions have to be examined not only in a theoretical sense, but also in consultation with supervisors or other persons who have the actual task of working with the employees who will be promoted or given the opportunity to fill vacancies.

Another part of the evaluation process is to review whether there are political or other reasons why an issue is on the bargaining table. It is possible that a particular demand for a job posting provision arises because of the imperatives of a national union office, rather than the local union membership. Similarly, there may have been a high-profile decision made in the operation, and a well-known or well-respected employee has been denied a position on grounds that have been perceived as unfair and discriminatory. As a result, an issue or problem may have attained far larger proportions than if it were viewed in the abstract. Thus, in making an evaluation, one has to examine not only how a demand would change the past practice, but also whether there are reasons, other than the merits of the matter, that have to be taken into account in deciding how to respond.

3. Resolution

The demand we have been discussing is a job posting provision. The problem has been identified, to the extent that the dimensions and application of the specific language have been reviewed, analyzed and assessed. The demand has been evaluated against the past history of the employer in filling job vacancies and the various factors the employer used when making its employment selections. Considerable time has been taken at the bargaining table and elsewhere, while the parties evaluated the reasons behind the demand and what its significance might be to the union itself, the union bargaining committee and the membership.

Now the task is to resolve the problem. How is this to be done? The simplest and easiest way, of course, is to agree to the demand and to include the proposed language in a new collective agreement. A number of years ago, I was present when my then law partner, a seasoned and able negotiator, was speaking to a young law student who was asking for the secret to obtaining a collective agreement. My partner looked at him and, in an imperious way, stated that if the student was prepared to follow one single rule, he could guarantee that collective agreement would be reached every time. The student was breathless and eager, and could hardly wait for the answer. My partner then said, "It's very simple, just give the bastards whatever they want!"

There are other ways to resolve the problem. The party that made a proposal may be persuaded to drop it. Why would it do this? There are a number of answers. The first and most obvious is that the proposer concludes it will not be possible to get agreement to its demand at the bargaining table, short of some kind of strike or confrontation, and, simply put, the proposal in question is not worth the price of alternative action. Another reason is that one side may package or put together several other collective agreement changes that it is prepared to agree to, but in return it may insist that the other side withdraw, for example, the job posting provision. That party must then decide whether the trade-off, that is, giving up the job posting provision in return for a number of other changes, is of sufficient value to merit a withdrawal of the job posting article. Another possibility is that the provision was put on the bargaining table not because there was any serious anticipation that the employer would agree to it, but because, tactically, it was felt the matter would create so many strong and negative negotiating reactions on the employer's part that its ultimate withdrawal from the bargaining table would provide a sense of major victory to the employer. Finally, the union may conclude that to obtain the job posting provision is necessarily a long-term process. As a result, the union may decide it will place the matter on the bargaining table and, this time, discuss the matter in great detail and do some conditioning to break down the employer's resistance to it. However, for the purpose of attempting to conclude a collective agreement within the present time period, the union may feel it will withdraw the demand, but in doing so it may warn the employer that the issue is still alive and will be at the top of the union's priority list in the next round of bargaining.

There is, of course, another way to resolve the problem, that is, by agreeing in part on the proposed language or establishing some alternative arrangement that will satisfy the parties, at least at this point in time. For example, the parties may agree that certain specified kinds of job openings will be posted. Or, there may be limitations on the categories of employees that can make application. Or, they may agree that anyone can signify his or her wish to be considered for a job by signing the job posting notice, but the employer has sole discretion in making selections. Or, they may agree that jobs will not be posted, but an individual employee may signify in writing his or her wish to be considered for a specific job, and such applications or notices of preference will be kept by the employer and considered when openings occur. All of these concepts, and there are others that can be developed with some imagination and creativity, are simply alternative ways of providing at least half a loaf to the party that made the particular demand. To extend the metaphor, the issue is how hungry is the party making the proposal, and how many slices, how thick do they have to be, and what kind of filling is needed, to satisfy that hunger.

The obvious question is "Why should that party accept half a loaf, or even a sandwich?" Again, there are many answers. A partial success may exceed a union bargaining committee's expectations, and may be more than sufficient to satisfy the membership. Another possibility is that, through the negotiating dialogue, the party making the proposal may begin to realize that a problem it thought was there, that is, the feeling of unfairness and discrimination in the awarding of appointments or jobs, has been exaggerated by the members, and the employer has in fact been acting responsibly. If a problem is found to be significantly less important, in proportion to its original dimensions, language that is less ambitious and far-reaching may be quite acceptable. Similarly, the consequence of implementation of the specific language that was proposed may be so serious that it may effectively create a larger problem than the one a proposed article is intended to resolve. Again, this perspective would arise only if the parties have had intense and frank discussions at the bargaining table to illuminate these concerns. Finally, a partial solution may be acceptable at this time because the long-term goal of the party that made the proposal is to assert more control over the employer's exercise of its managerial rights. A particular job posting provision may be viewed simply as one item in an incremental move in the direction of control. If that party's interest is in generating momentum in a given direction, its acceptance of a job posting provision that is substantially less than it originally proposed may meet its long-term objective, because what is more important than the specific steps is moving in a defined direction towards the goal of control.

4. Rules for the Negotiator

To be able to negotiate effectively, a person requires both the ability to analyze and the capacity to act quickly and decisively in an intuitive or instinctive way. Some negotiating skills cannot be learned, as they are a reflection of the presence or absence of the innate qualities of the individual. On the other hand, there is no such thing as a born negotiator, that is, a person who is an effective negotiator without any prior learning or training on the subject. Negotiating skills are, to a large degree, an acquired faculty. Here is a list of the ten most important rules to follow as a negotiator:

Rule 1. Bargain positively.

At all times you should appear confident and assured at the bargaining table. You should assume a bargaining attitude of a positive nature. From the very start of bargaining you should make it clear that it is your intention to reach an acceptable collective agreement, and you have every expectation that with hard work and goodwill such an aim can be achieved. In a real sense, you are a salesperson. You are selling two things; the first is yourself, and the second is the position of the party that you are representing on a particular issue. If you cannot sell yourself, it is unlikely you can persuade the other side to agree with you on an issue. Your manner, demeanour, attitude and conduct at the bargaining table should project you as a person who can be both trusted and believed.

Rule 2. Be objective.

Since you are at the bargaining table for the purpose of trying to get someone to agree with you, it is important to be clear-minded about what the other party needs, and then to find a way to package a deal it can accept. It should be understood that, on most occasions, an agreement on a given issue requires either or both parties to change their original opinion. It is also the case that many collective bargaining tables become covered with a lot of emotional blood which has been spilled from all of the participants. People get angry and hostile because of the nature of the issues they are dealing with, and the positions each party holds in relation to those who are affected by them. In the midst of this turmoil it is critical to keep your emotional feet on the ground and to maintain your objectivity. If you do not do so, you will lose your capacity to think clearly, and you will lose your perspective.

Rule 3. Never assume knowledge on the part of others.

Most of us have a tendency to assume others know a good deal about a great many subjects when in fact their information is limited. As a result, arguments in support of a position may not have any persuasive value because they are not understood. This is not because the arguments are phrased poorly, or are flawed. What may happen is that the person making an argument assumes the listeners know more than they in fact do. For example, some management persons have a detailed knowledge of corporate finance and accounting principles. If a presentation is being made on the basis of an employer's inability to pay as a result of economic events and circumstances, the person making the presentation has to be careful to use words, terms and concepts that are clearly understood by the persons being addressed.

Let me give two examples. The first involves a bargaining session where a company controller was reviewing the sad state of the employer's economic affairs. He stated that the gross sales in the previous year had been in excess of $1.5 million. He then went on to explain that the employer was broke, and therefore it had no money available to pay the wages that were being demanded. At no time did he explain what profits were, or that the money obtained by selling the product was the source of funds for paying all of the employer's bills, from rent and fuel to wages and employee benefits. Needless to say, the union bargaining committee, unsophisticated in economic theory, refused to believe anything it was told about the employer's ability to pay.

The second example results from the Canadian government's anti-inflation program, AIB, under Prime Minister Trudeau, and the detailed costing forms that employers had to fill out in order to determine total compensation. This exercise taught many persons more than they ever wanted to know about the costing of employment benefits. However, with time, some imaginative negotiators on the employer's side began to share this information at the bargaining table. As a result, many union bargaining committees were startled to find that their demands would cost so much. What was especially striking was that so many employers thought the union already knew the cost of what it was proposing.

Rule 4. Always maintain your integrity.

Obviously, you do not want to lie or cheat at the bargaining table — not only because you may get caught, but a mere suspicion will cheapen the coinage of what you offer as a negotiator. If you distort or misrepresent information, you will probably be found out. But the impact is not so much on you in a personal sense as on the party you are representing. Thus, you both lose.

Rule 5. Negotiators are real people, and real people are no different from you and me.

People negotiate collective agreements, and they all have the incurable habit of behaving like human beings. Put aside your biases and prejudices, recognize all of you are going to be spending time together and somehow, at some level, you are going to have to communicate. So try to meet the other negotiators at some level, however superficial. Do not be negative or defensive about this. Treat the situation positively. Be sure you can understand the individuals you are negotiating with, not only what motivates and drives them, but also how they can be moved or challenged or, in a word, manipulated. This is not intended as a critical or pejorative concept. As a negotiator you have an objective and that is to persuade others to agree with you, to give up things they want, and to give you things they do not want to give. The question then is not "What?" but "How?" The answer is "It depends" — on the way in which the negotiators are able to relate to each other, for better or for worse, in bad temper or good, until the end of the bargaining when they can part.

Rule 6. Watch your language.

In your choice of words, in your selection of phrases, be clear and careful. In your search for clarity, focus on finding words that express exactly what you want to say. Sometimes you may want to be vague and discursive, perhaps to buy time and to provide some negotiating breathing room. On these occasions, a fog of words that gently settles over the bargaining table can have a relaxing and soothing effect. The point is that words should be used in a purposeful way. Some words should not be used, in particular the word "never". Never is too long a time, even in these inflationary days. It is too large and indigestible a word to swallow easily. When you use words like this, you block yourself into a negotiating corner. More importantly, it is all so unnecessary. Speak clearly and carefully, and if you cannot find the right word to express what you want to say, keep quiet.

Rule 7. Keep your perspective.

Any one set of negotiations is simply part of a continuing relationship between the particular parties. What is said and done at the bargaining table, the feelings and emotions generated between the people involved, may last long after the issues themselves. The parties do not stop dealing with each other merely because they have settled their collective agreement dispute. The individuals will be back working with each other as soon as the meetings have concluded and the collective agreement has been signed. Soon, in fact all too soon, they will be negotiating together again. Negotiators' memories, like elephants', are long-lived.

Rule 8. Don't lose your sense of humour.

Humour is often the grease that keeps the negotiating wheels turning. A tense, troubled atmosphere may be lightened with a quip or story. In this, as in everything else at the bargaining table, a story intended to be funny but told at the wrong time, or a story that is in bad taste in relation to the people at the bargaining table, will if anything tighten the tension. On the other hand, humour helps to give proper perspective to the issues and to the attitudes of the participants. You don't want to be a smart-ass, and your role is not that of a comedian. However, a dose of humour, used sparingly, will go down well.

Rule 9. Remember why you are there.

The object of negotiations is to reach agreement. An enthusiasm for combat should not gloss over the fact that negotiations are not a game. Let me repeat; both the object and the consequences on other people are too serious for negotiations ever to be considered a game. It is all too easy for even an experienced negotiator to get caught up in the flow of the action and to forget about the main objective, which is to get a settlement. If your interest is in exercising your own ego, in winning for your own sake, in demonstrating your own prowess, you are going to mess up when you walk into the negotiating room. You are there to negotiate, not to play games.

Rule 10. Try to learn each time you negotiate.

Much of your time at the bargaining table is spent making judgments on matters large and small. Most of these are fine judgments, where there is no right or wrong answer. A negotiator is seldom working with concepts that are black or white. In most cases, the only coloration is a series of shades of grey. Some of the judgments that are made will necessarily turn out to be incorrect. If you find you made a negotiating error (and all negotiators make mistakes, if only because they are human), accept what happened, recognize your mistake, swallow hard, and learn from what you did or did not do. If a bargaining mistake is made, you must learn to live with it, and not repeat it.

Chapter 5

Negotiating Sessions

1. First Negotiating Session

The first bargaining session is much more than a formality. What takes place may set the tone for the following meetings and, in some cases, for the entire negotiations. First impressions may be lasting, and the perceptions of the negotiators, like glue, may stick.

In the normal course of events, the union would have given the employer written notice of its intent to bargain. On receipt of this notice the respective spokespersons would confer to discuss when and where the first bargaining meeting will take place. The union bargaining committee would have held meetings with the union membership to draft proposals for amendments to the existing collective agreement. If the collective agreement is a first agreement, the union bargaining committee would have prepared a proposed draft collective agreement for presentation to the employer.

The primary purpose of the first meeting is for the employer to receive the union collective agreement demands on which the subsequent negotiations will be based. Another important purpose, however, is for the negotiators to get to meet each other — often for the first time — and for them to establish some ground rules and schedules for the next meetings.

Quite obviously, the members of the two committees are wary of each other, and uncertain as to what the negotiating future holds. Each will be sizing up the other, trying to get a sense of the attitudes, temperaments and ideological baggage being brought to the bargaining table. For example, is someone showing an aggressive attitude and carrying a negotiating chip on the shoulder? Who is doing most of the talking? What is the body language of the negotiators? Are there any signs of tension evident?

If, from the start of the first meeting, the negotiators seem relaxed with each other and able to talk together with some measure of ease and, even more importantly, are willing to listen to each other, that alone may get the negotiations off on the right foot. On the other hand, if someone is scornful or sarcastic, especially in a personal way, someone else will necessarily feel obliged to counter-attack, making it difficult for the parties to speak to each other in any constructive way. It is literally true that if you can't talk together, you can't negotiate.

As a result, each member of the employer negotiating team should introduce himself or herself to each member of the union bargaining committee. Depending on the style and manner of the people present, there is usually an exchange of small talk and pleasantries before the start of the business part of the meeting. The union bargaining committee should then be invited to table its demands, and allowed to make its presentation in whatever form and manner it chooses. Presumably, the demands will be in written form and may form a bundle of papers many pages in length. The union representative has the floor. It is his or her show. Let the union representative make his or her remarks with whatever colour and exaggerations he or she wishes. But listen; listen hard. You can learn so much if you open your ears and focus your mind on not just what is being said, but how it is being said. Is the presentation factual? Inflammatory? Is it a fighting speech or conciliatory and constructive?

The union bargaining committee members should be permitted and, indeed, invited to say whatever they wish in order to explain, support or amplify the proposals that are being tabled with the employer. They should not be interrupted or questioned in detail, but they should be heard out.

At the completion of the general remarks of the union representative, the employer spokesperson should state that it is the intention of the employer negotiating team to give careful consideration to all of the union demands, and to make no comment on the demands until they have been examined in detail. The discussion should then turn to arranging the date for the next meeting or meetings, including details of location, time, and other similar matters. If the employer intends to submit proposals of its own, such as language amendments to the collective agreement, it is a good idea to tell the union bargaining committee of this fact at the first meeting, perhaps coupled with an undertaking by the employer spokesperson that such proposals will be tabled at the next following meeting. Or, if they cannot be prepared by that date, when they can be expected.

Perhaps a word of explanation is in order. The employer negotiating team may table at any time counter-proposals in response to union demands, accepting part of the union demands or suggesting changes, or both. However, apart from and despite the union demands, the employer may have decided that certain articles of the existing collective agreement are unworkable, or need change. Before the first negotiating meeting, the employer negotiating team should have thought through the tactical advantages of making proposals of its own, and what these specific proposals should contain. These proposals should not be held back until negotiations are largely completed, but the employer spokesperson should tell the union bargaining committee at the earliest appropriate opportunity that the employer intends to make its own proposals. If the employer spokesperson keeps quiet and then tries to spring a negotiating ambush, this will antagonize the other side, doom any serious consideration of the proposals, and cause a cry of bargaining in bad faith. To repeat, it is proper, and in many cases advisable, for the employer to seek whatever collective agreement changes, deletions or additions it thinks are necessary, but in doing so it should tell the union bargaining committee of its intentions early, not late.

2. Second Negotiating Session

The interval of time between the first and second negotiating sessions must be sufficient to allow the employer negotiating team time to examine the substance and details of the union demands. On any economic matters, the employer will also need time to attempt to try and figure out the cost of the demands, both individually and as a composite number.

The primary purpose of the second negotiating session is to clarify the intent and meaning of the individual union demands, and to try and bring out both the reasons and the motivation for each. The employer spokesperson must walk a fine line between questioning and attacking, probing and arguing.

As stated, before the second meeting begins, the members of the employer negotiating team should have studied the specifics of each of the union demands. Depending on the clarity of the wording, in some instances they may be uncertain or unsure what is intended by a demand, or how it would work. In other cases, the language may be clear and explicit, but they can only guess as to the reasons for the demand being made. Rather than beginning the meeting by attacking the merits of a particular collective agreement demand, the employer spokesperson should ask the union bargaining committee members to say why they feel a change is necessary, or needed, in the current language of the collective agreement.

It has been stated by some arbitrators that one of the purposes of holding grievance meetings in resolving rights disputes under a collective agreement is to provide an opportunity to the parties to "ventilate". The expression is even more apt at the bargaining table. There are many instances where collective agreement demands are framed in one way, but are in fact a reflection of a totally different problem. If an employer negotiating team probes the reasons for the making of a demand, it may become clear from the discussion that the union bargaining committee in reality is concerned with a different matter, for example, one that requires no change in the collective agreement language, but does require another method of implementation by the employer. In other words, a discussion of the reasons and difficulties that brought about a demand may enable the parties to identify a real problem, which may or may not be identified in the demand. Simply put, you cannot solve a problem that you cannot either identify or understand.

It is also a fact that some demands are directed at serving a social or political purpose. Such demands may be made in order to satisfy those of the union membership who are agitated about a particular subject, for example, pay equity, or safety in the workplace. The bargaining table may be used as an opportunity to express frustration, to demand action and attention. It is the fact that the message has been given that is important, especially if it is done with heat and passion. In due course, the union bargaining committee members can report back how angrily they dumped all over the employer negotiating team, and this, rather than concrete acts, may be what is needed.

Since the negotiations have just begun, the employer spokesperson should avoid making direct criticism of any specific collective agreement demand, and should not reveal the employer's position on any particular demand. Before an employer can intelligently respond, it must first fully understand the intent and meaning of each of the collective agreement demands, the reasons for each demand, how it will apply, and to whom. As a consequence, the role of the members of the employer negotiating team is multi-purpose: to question, to listen and to record what is said by the union bargaining committee on each demand.

Taking each of these points in turn, questions should not be posed by all members of the employer negotiating team, but are best asked by the employer spokesperson. Questions should not be put in an aggressive, argumentative fashion, but phrased so as to bring about a response and to elicit information from the other side. As to the importance of listening, it is a rare but significant skill. A union representative who speaks should be heard and not interrupted, even if the remarks seem wandering or tedious. Courtesy at the bargaining table is as essential to the process as it is to any other part of life. As for the taking of notes, someone on the employer negotiating team should be assigned the task of recording the substance of what is being said. The notes should be as accurate and as complete as possible concerning the respective arguments and positions being advanced at each step. The union bargaining committee will doubtless make the same arrangement, so that each side will have a running report of the major dialogue at each of the bargaining sessions. It is even more helpful if the note-taker is able to put down observations, hopefully objectively, about the mood, demeanour and reactive signposts of the members of the other committee. What is sometimes as important as what is said is the manner of saying it, and how people react. For example, does it appear that someone disagrees? Is someone visibly angry?

If the parties are negotiating a first collective agreement, the employer may want to proceed on a quite different negotiating tack than is the case with respect to a renewal collective agreement. It can be assumed that at the first negotiating meeting the union will table a full collective agreement proposal, which will include all of the language matters on which the union intends to bargain, together with some, if not all, of the economic items. The employer has, essentially, two options it can follow. In the first place, it can choose to respond to the union's draft collective agreement, and negotiate on that draft, by suggesting amendments, changes, or deletions to the union's proposed language. The second option for the employer is to prepare its own draft collective agreement for presentation to the union at the second bargaining session. Such a draft collective agreement may or may not include economic items. Most commonly, it will provide the employer's proposal for the non-economic language only. If this latter option is selected, the employer spokesperson should table the draft collective agreement, together with a statement that this represents the employer's complete response to the corresponding provisions of the union's draft collective agreement. The employer would have as its objective persuading the union bargaining committee to negotiate on the basis of the employer's draft collective agreement. If this is acceptable to the union bargaining committee, the employer should then avoid any further reference to, or discussion of, the union's draft collective agreement. The reasoning here is simple to state but difficult to implement. It is always best to get the other side to respond to your bargaining issues as you have defined them. That way you have much more control over both the substance and the pace of the bargaining.

In most sets of negotiations, the parties agree at an early stage to separate economic and non-economic items, and to deal with non-economic matters first. This is generally the case whether a first collective agreement is involved or the renewal of an existing collective agreement. The time to reach such an understanding is at this meeting, and the subject should be openly discussed so that both parties can have some idea of the ground rules for subsequent meetings. Obviously, confusion is seldom a help to negotiators, and discussing together economic and non-economic issues, especially in bulk, makes the bargaining mixture somewhat indigestible, because the considerations are so different in judging seniority issues at the same time as an appropriate wage increase.

A further matter that should be covered at this point is the question of secrecy concerning what is said and done at the bargaining table. The negotiations may be protracted over a long period of time, and it may be almost impossible to avoid some discussion with outsiders on what is happening at the bargaining table. Nevertheless, if the bargaining process is going to work, the parties must be able to talk openly and frankly, in a candid manner, without fear that their words will be reported to others. Most parties to collective bargaining negotiations agree on the wisdom of not revealing what is happening during bargaining, at least as long as negotiations are continuing to make progress. In some cases, the position of the union is to request a complete ban on statements to employees from both sides until a strike is called. The employer negotiating team should be cautious in agreeing to such an arrangement and, in any event, should protect itself by insisting that if the ban is broken by the union, the employer will be free to advise its employees of what has transpired in negotiations.

Simply put, the second negotiating session should be an intensive question and answer exchange, combined with a discussion and agreement as to how the following session is to be conducted, and what items are to be discussed at that time. The meeting should then be adjourned, hopefully on an upbeat note, with a recognition that at least the parties are starting to talk together. It is difficult to resolve something if you can't talk to or with the other negotiating party. In that sense, talking must be understood as a process of reaching out to make contact, and then one builds on that foundation.

3. Third and Subsequent Bargaining Sessions

In these sessions one can expect the employer negotiating team to begin to provide direct responses to at least some of the union demands. Not only are the responses important in themselves, but the manner of making them is almost of equal importance in establishing negotiating momentum and setting a constructive tone and atmosphere.

Presumably, in preparing for the negotiations, the employer negotiating team will have assembled and analyzed information, both from its own sources and outside comparisons, on the various collective agreement articles put in issue by the union. Such information should be used to assess the union demands on a compensation basis, and to determine an appropriate response. Thus, at this point in the bargaining, the preparation has been done, the demands have been tabled and explained, and now the parties start to move, carefully and tentatively, toward each other.

The parties have to start somewhere. The practice, particularly from an employer's viewpoint, is to begin with the non-economic matters. Why? The language determines the amount of flexibility, which in turn affects the economic capacity of the employer. In addition, once the cost items are agreed on, there is no leverage left to the employer on the remaining matters. In addressing these non-economic matters, the employer spokesperson should identify them by article number, and a list should be compiled for use by both sides, so there will be no misunderstanding as to which items are to be considered as economic and which are not. Once this is done, the employer spokesperson can proceed to respond to each of the language issues in turn, by advising the union bargaining committee whether a specific article is acceptable to the employer or is not acceptable, or whether the employer intends to make a counter-proposal on that specific matter. Each of the language issues can be reviewed in sequence, so that the union bargaining committee can be directly informed of the position of the employer on each of the language issues. Basically, there are four options to consider on each item: Yes! No! Set Aside and Discuss Later! and Counter-proposal!

An alternative method is for the employer spokesperson to select one of the articles and state the employer's position on that article and the rationale for taking that position. The article, but only that article, is then reviewed and discussed in detail. Here, the notion is that this matter is to be isolated and focused on without reference to any other provisions of the collective agreement.

Sometimes, the choice of these two methods is dictated in part by the time pressures on either or both parties, and sometimes it is a matter of priority and tactics. If the parties are pushing hard for an early agreement, the employer's position should be given on all of the language issues at the same time, since this will necessarily force the pace. On the other hand, if the parties are still feeling each other out and want to be cautious, particularly if there is clearly a matter in dispute they anticipate will be a major controversy, it is best they take the single issue approach, rather than a package or multiple approach.

Obviously, if the union demand is acceptable without change, the discussions on that matter are ended, provided the employer spokesperson has clearly and unequivocally assented to the demand. It is a good practice for the parties to write down in their own notes that agreement has been reached on that demand. Depending in part on the degree of mutual trust — or mistrust — between the parties, it is also a wise move to have the two spokespersons initial a copy of the language that has been agreed upon. The purpose of this is obvious. There may be dozens of collective agreement changes agreed to in negotiations that may extend over many meetings and a number of months. When the final collective agreement is ready to be signed, the parties will want to avoid any arguments about what was agreed on and what was not. If they rely on their memories or their own notes, they may well have gaps or statements that are incomplete. If they have left a precise paper trail, they can easily reconstruct the words and the undertakings.

It is equally obvious that a specific demand, say, a change in the way seniority is accumulated, may be acceptable in principle or in part, but the employer may want different or revised language to that proposed by the union. If this is the case, the employer should first draft, and then table, the actual language that it is prepared to accept, together with an outline of why the union provision needs to be changed or modified. Just as in the case of first collective agreement negotiations, it is preferable to persuade the other side to negotiate from your draft rather than from its draft. However, it is not enough simply to hand over proposed counter-language without some explanation as to why this is being done and what the revisions are intended to accomplish. The employer spokesperson should make a statement to the effect that the employer negotiating team has carefully studied the union demand, and while there are some elements that it can agree with, it feels the language can be better expressed in another way. It should be made clear that the employer's proposed draft has been prepared to reflect the union concerns, as expressed in the previous sessions, as well as the employer's requirements. The tone should be upbeat and positive, so that the union bargaining committee can feel it has accomplished its objective, except to the extent that the employer's language has modified things.

In a word, the objective is to establish "momentum". This means that the parties will begin to feel that negotiations are moving, to the extent that certain matters are agreed and others dropped, so as to narrow and eventually close the negotiating gap. If all of the union demands are totally unacceptable, there is no way to create the appearance of agreement, since there is none. If some or any part of the union demands are acceptable, the employer spokesperson can review and address each demand as a separate matter, or, alternatively, accept with a price tag, that is, by attaching to the employer's acceptance a condition that some other item in the union demands be withdrawn or changed. The extent of the progress to be made by the parties from this point will depend upon continuing to move the negotiations forward, and agreement being reached on certain items, arranging the withdrawal of others, together with the modification of yet others. As long as changes in the respective bargaining positions are either being made or being considered, there is justification for continuing to meet. However, once the parties have reached an impasse and their negotiating positions have become locked and rigid, both the reality and the perception of progress disappears and a sense of futility may set in. When this happens, the emotional mind-set that progress has stopped can be more difficult to overcome than the issue itself. For this reason, most experienced negotiators try very hard to create some feeling of optimism in the opposite committee.

One of the questions that may be asked is how to react to the presence of verbal abuse or insults. Collective bargaining negotiations frequently take place in an emotionally charged climate, and passions may run high and tempers become short. While it is a generalization, it is the case that a businesslike and professional attitude is now more common at the bargaining table than it was a few years ago, but of course, there are occasions when one or more negotiators explode, at least verbally.

One very human reaction of a negotiator faced with a torrent of abuse from someone sitting across a bargaining table is to respond in kind. This will have the effect of generating even more aggressive words, and escalating the confrontation. The more effective way to handle the situation is for the person who is being abused and attacked to interrupt the tirade and, quite literally, get up and leave the room. The negotiator on the receiving end should state that when the other person is prepared to talk rationally and negotiate properly, the meeting can be resumed. Obviously, all members of that committee should also leave the room, and if necessary, the meeting should be discontinued for an appropriate cooling-off period. In any event, a verbally violent and personal attack by one person should not be matched by an equally aggressive response from another person, or the negotiations will degenerate into a shouting match. I once received some sound advice from a union colleague. "Never get into a urinating contest with a skunk!" Sage, if indelicate, advice.

4. Bargaining in Bad Faith

Under the legislative scheme of the *Canada Labour Code* as well as the labour relations statutes of all provinces, both parties to negotiations are under a statutory duty to bargain in good faith with a view to entering into a collective agreement. In recent years there have been instances where the appropriate labour relations board was called upon to review the negotiating conduct of a party to see if this duty had been breached. Recently, and regrettably, there have been efforts made by some parties to claim a breach of this statutory duty as a regular part of their negotiating tactics, almost as a matter of routine.

While it is not my purpose to provide a full legal treatise on the principles of what constitutes bargaining in bad faith, it is important to remember that the labour relations boards are increasingly interventionist in their approach to most labour relations matters, in particular, what they perceive to be bad faith bargaining. Consequently, there is more likelihood at this time that a tribunal will be prepared not only to examine the negotiating conduct of one or both parties, but perhaps more importantly, to inject itself into the bargaining process by means of determining an appropriate remedy in the event that a breach of the statutory duty has been found. For example, a board may be persuaded, through the mechanism of an unfair labour practice charge, that the bargaining in question has been conducted in bad faith. If so, the board has available a number of weapons in its arsenal of remedies. Offers that have been withdrawn can be ordered to be revived, collective agreements that have been repudiated can be directed to be signed, damages can be assessed, bargaining rights extended, and so on. Put simply, bad faith bargaining is treated harshly, since it violates the very foundation of the labour relations statute — the fostering and encouragement of collective bargaining.

It is important to recognize that a tribunal will review the entire negotiating conduct in determining whether bad faith exists. In other words, if there have been a number of individual circumstances that in the aggregate disclose a pattern of bad faith, the board will find a violation of the Act, even though each of the individual circumstances standing alone would not be sufficient to disclose such a pattern or constitute a violation in itself. In addition, because this statutory provision and the seriousness with which it is viewed is more widely known, a party in negotiating difficulty may be tempted to try to involve the labour relations board in the negotiating process, in the hope that the threat of public hearings and the possibility of invoking the board's sanction will assist that party, whether bad faith has been disclosed or not. In short, one party may attempt to use this mechanism as a bargaining lever against the other side, particularly if the applicant is having little success in achieving its collective bargaining aims.

The increased reliance on this action has caused another difficulty that should be mentioned. So as to avoid any insinuation of bad faith, some parties have overreacted and have been overly cautious in their dealings. For instance, one Ontario case on the subject states it is bad faith bargaining for one party to refuse to discuss or debate the other party's proposals or to hear that party's rationale or presentation of the proposals, and has ruled that there must be some dialogue between the parties on the subject. There are occasions when one negotiating side may be totally opposed to a given position, and anxious to avoid leaving any impression that it may be flexible or that it may, somehow, reconsider. If the spokesperson for that party states, as soon as the matter is introduced, that there is no point in having any discussion or dialogue on the matter because the party's position is fixed and will not change, this could be viewed as bad faith bargaining. On the other hand, the very essence of bargaining in good faith is to be frank and candid in expressing views on the matter or matters being negotiated. Thus, the negotiators in some cases may feel under a legal restraint, and unable to speak clearly and unequivocally.

In Ontario a new dimension has been added with the creation of what is called "first contract arbitration". Under section 40a of the *Labour Relations Act*, where the parties are unable to reach a first collective agreement and the conciliation procedure has been exhausted, either party may apply to the board to direct the settlement of the collective agreement by an arbitrator. It is not a requirement to the appointment of an arbitrator that the board find a failure to bargain in good faith. However, the board must find a "refusal to recognize the bargaining authority of the trade union" or that the bargaining was unsuccessful because of the "uncompromising nature of any bargaining position . . . without reasonable justification" or that there was a failure to make "reasonable or expeditious efforts to conclude a collective agreement".

If there is an affirmative finding on one or more of these grounds, a board of arbitration is appointed, unless the parties agree to allow the Ontario Labour Relations Board to settle the collective agreement. The matters previously agreed to in the bargaining, plus the remaining issues that are still in dispute and determined by the arbitrator, then make up the new collective agreement imposed on the parties. The combination of the matters already agreed on and the arbitrated provisions constitutes a binding collective agreement.

When the section was first enacted, it was anticipated by many that it would be widely used. As a practical matter, its presence has acted as a spur to most parties to resolve their own collective agreement differences. Ironically, many union persons recognize that a collective agreement imposed by arbitration is not a good way to start a relationship. Arbitrated collective agreements are like forced marriages — they might work but the odds are against them.

Nevertheless, the section is there; it is a shadow on the bargaining landscape. It is a threat only to the unreasonably intransigent bargainer, the party that walks the edge of bad faith bargaining. It should be repeated, however, that it applies only to first collective agreement disputes, and not to the renewal of any collective agreement.

Chapter 6

Conciliation

In all jurisdictions in Canada, a lawful strike or lock-out may take place only after conciliation. This is in contrast to the American collective bargaining procedure which includes a voluntary (instead of compulsory) conciliation stage and where strikes may take place in certain prescribed situations even when the collective agreement has not expired.

In most jurisdictions, the conciliation stage is divided into two phases by statute. The first phase is the appointment of a conciliation officer who meets with the parties in an effort to settle the dispute. The second phase is only a matter of form, apart from the federal government system. It provides for the appointment of a conciliation board which not only will conciliate between the parties but, if a settlement is not attained, will make recommendations to the parties. Over the years conciliation boards have been abandoned, except in the federal jurisdiction — and even there they are rare. Partly as a consequence of this fact, a hybrid mechanism has been created, called mediation, which is really conciliation but during acute crisis, either just before or during a strike. The subject of mediation is discussed in the next chapter.

1. The Conciliation Officer

The first premise in any collective bargaining model is that the parties should attempt to resolve their differences by themselves without outside interference. If the parties have met and an impasse has been reached, the notion is that it is in the public interest that a respected and neutral person, called a conciliation officer, conduct a meeting of the parties in order to help them to find common ground and to assist them by bringing them together. Since a conciliation officer is employed by the government, and since the overall policy direction of any government is to reduce both the occurrences and consequences of economic confrontations, or, more bluntly, strikes and lock-outs, the purpose of a conciliation officer as a person charged with the duty to help the parties to help themselves is consistent with advancing the public interest.

Over the past few decades the provinces and the federal government have trained and developed a group of experienced and able conciliation officers. These men and women have made an invaluable contribution to the labour relations community and to the public at large. While styles and approaches differ with the individual, there are certain characteristics that are common to all effective conciliation officers.

(a) Characteristics of a conciliator

The first quality that a conciliation officer brings to the bargaining table is objectivity. A conciliation officer has no personal axe to grind in a dispute and can cut through the self-serving rhetoric and emotionalism which may have clouded the judgments of the parties. It is an all too common problem for any negotiator to be caught up in the intricacies and nit-picking of a particular dispute and to ignore the real issues and problems. In short, the negotiator loses sight of the negotiating forest for the trees. It is common for negotiators to be so involved in the gamesmanship of the negotiations, the cut and thrust of the discussion, that they are unable or unwilling to see a way to reach a settlement, or to realize they are in fact debating and not negotiating. A conciliation officer, on the other hand, can approach the issues and the parties with a clear eye and with the opportunity to assess the merits of the positions without emotionalism and with no personal stake in what may be achieved as a settlement. The fact that a conciliation officer does not have to live with the consequences of a settlement is a spur to the officer's objectivity; it is also a factor that the unwary negotiator will ignore at his or her peril.

The second quality is experience. With time, a conciliation officer can be expected to be involved in a large number of disputes which may assist him or her in finding a solution for a particular set of parties. In part because of that same experience, the officer may be able to bring to the parties examples of other settlements or analogous situations which can be used as examples or models for a settlement. Equally important, over a period of time a conciliation officer builds up a number of personal contacts with negotiators on both sides that can be used as an aid to open communication channels for the parties. An experienced officer knows who to talk to as well as who can be believed and who can be trusted.

A third quality is knowledge — an instinct and feel for the negotiation process. A skilled conciliation officer can push and prod, bluster and bluff, cajole and connive, soothe and soften, sometimes all in the same meeting. The real art is knowing which technique to employ, to whom and when, in order to get reluctant negotiators to reach agreement.

A fourth quality is integrity. The conciliation officer's role not only requires neutrality in the sense that he or she should not prefer or side with any one of the parties, but also requires that the officer be seen to be neutral.

To put this another way, the parties must be prepared to confide to an officer what their real positions are in contrast to their formal negotiating positions. The parties must have assurance that an officer will not abuse the positions of either party and that their confidences will be respected. If an officer does not appear to have a strong sense of professional integrity, the parties will not be prepared to talk frankly and the officer will be unable to work effectively. Without mutual trust between the negotiators and the conciliation officer, the conciliation process simply will not function, but the officer must earn the confidence of the parties.

(b) Appointment of a conciliation officer

The mechanical steps to obtain the appointment of a conciliation officer are straightforward. Once the parties have met on their own and bargained, either the union or the employer may apply to the respective Ministry of Labour by completing the appropriate application form and requesting that a conciliation officer be appointed. The only two conditions precedent for the making of such an application are that proper notice to bargain must have been given by one party to the other and the parties must have met at least once. There are no time limits as to when the application must be made and no limitation on the number of bargaining meetings the parties may have on their own. An application may be made by either an employer or a union, whether the other side consents or not. A copy of the application must be sent to the other side at the same time that it is forwarded to the Ministry, but the applicant is not required to inform the other party that it is intending to apply before it goes ahead and does so.

The appointment of a conciliation officer is a matter of ministerial discretion, at least in theory. In practice, an application is invariably granted unless the employer claims that the applicant union does not have the lawful right to bargain for the employees involved in the application. For example, if there are several plants operated by an employer, some of which are certified and some of which are not, and a union seeks the appointment of a conciliation officer to deal with a dispute concerning a plant that is not covered by the certification order or recognition clause of the existing collective agreement, the employer could object to the appointment insofar as it affects the uncertified plant. In this event, if the union refused to amend the application, the matter would be referred to the labour relations board for a ruling as to whether the union has the bargaining rights in the plant or plants concerned, and what is the precise scope of the bargaining rights. The ruling of the board would be accepted as a final determination of that issue, and the officer's appointment would be limited accordingly.

In some instances, the timing of an application for the appointment of a conciliation officer is of important tactical advantage to one party or the other. For instance, the union may wish to bring negotiations to a crisis quickly because the employees are restless, while the employer may be anxious to build up inventory, fill its orders and delay the negotiating process as long as possible so it can continue to operate. Thus, the union may make application at an early date, even though only one or perhaps two meetings have been held between the parties. The employer, trying to gain operating time and profits, may respond to the application by claiming that the application is premature, on the grounds that a collective bargaining dispute has not been reached and the parties should be given further time to meet on their own before an appointment is made.

It is the policy of most Ministries of Labour to avoid any adjudication on the question of whether or not there is a real impasse at this stage, since this is not a condition for the appointment. The application will normally be granted and the conciliation officer may then direct the parties to meet and bargain on their own and report their progress. At best, the application will be held up and the appointment delayed for a few days while the parties are contacted and consulted as to their positions. In any event, once an application is made, a party that is objecting to the appointment must reply to the application and make the appropriate representations within the prescribed time period. In Ontario this period is five days from the receipt of the application. If no objections to the application are made within this time period, the application will be granted in the normal way. In most cases no objection is made, and in many instances the application is made either jointly or by one party applying with the other side's consent recorded in the application itself.

Although an application has been made and a conciliation officer has been appointed, there is nothing to preclude the parties from meeting on their own and continuing to bargain. If an officer has already been appointed, it is only common sense that he or she be informed if the parties intend to meet to try to settle the dispute without the involvement or attendance of the officer. Such direct meetings may be useful if there are a large number of matters in dispute. The meetings may not bring a complete settlement but may narrow the dispute and resolve some of the contentious issues. This would clear the negotiating decks so that only a handful of key issues would remain to be conciliated. On the other hand, there are obvious hurdles to negotiating seriously when a conciliation officer has been appointed and the parties are waiting for a conciliation meeting to be held. One of the parties may want to make significant concessions on a given point or points in dispute because it suits its bargaining timetable or agenda. On the other hand, the natural temptation for the other side is to listen to what has been said, accept those proposals that are irresistibly attractive, but feel that a conciliation officer may be able to extract even more when a conciliation meeting takes place. Simply put, a party can always accept a proposal later; it has nothing to lose by letting a conciliation officer call a meeting to see if further concessions can be extracted. Nevertheless, if both parties are under pressure to bring about an early settlement and avoid increasing the tension, there may be merit in bargaining directly despite the appointment of a conciliation officer. If, however, there is no mutual interest in the bargaining, or if only one of the parties is genuinely anxious to reach an early settlement, it is unlikely the other side will be prepared to make any major changes in its position without using a meeting with the officer as leverage, especially if one party has communicated its uneasiness to the other side. An experienced negotiator will not only react to the bargaining strengths of his or her own side but, of equal importance, will also take advantage of the limitations or imperatives of the other side. A bargainer reveals his or her weakness at his or her peril, and the greater the weakness, be it real or perceived, the higher the cost.

The selection of a conciliation officer is made by the administrative officials of the respective Ministry of Labour. As a matter of practical convenience, either or both parties may request that a particular conciliation officer be appointed, especially if such individual has worked successfully with the parties in previous collective bargaining disputes. In such a case the conciliation officer will have acquired knowledge and experience of the industry and of the particular operation, and will have established a bond of credibility with the parties which in turn will make the officer's task easier.

Once appointed, a conciliation officer will normally get in touch with the parties by telephone to establish a mutually agreeable time and place for a meeting. The timing and location of the meeting may ultimately be decided by the officer in consultation with the parties, but it normally is held either in the Ministry of Labour offices or in some neutral location such as a hotel or other place of public accommodation.

(c) Role

It must be stressed that a conciliation officer is appointed for the purpose of assisting the parties in reaching a settlement of their own collective bargaining dispute. It is not the function of an officer to make judgments on the merits of the bargaining positions of either or both parties. The parties must make their own collective bargaining decisions; an officer's role is to try and find a formula that will enable both parties to achieve enough of their collective bargaining aims that they will decide to conclude their dispute. The terms of the resulting collective agreement are binding on the parties to it — not on the conciliation officer. If an employer is persuaded to pay too much, it is the employer who must live with the consequences — not the conciliation officer. If a union bargaining committee withdraws certain major demands of the union membership, the fallout will descend on the committee — not the conciliation officer.

An officer may make suggestions to either or both sides, but such suggestions, even if loosely termed "recommendations", are not binding and can be accepted or ignored as the parties choose. Thus, each party must be prepared to accept responsibility for its own actions, and an officer is not obliged to analyze or explain to one party the implications or consequences of what the other party has proposed. For example, an officer may bring to one party an economic proposal and that party may accept the proposal without recognizing the cost involved or what it means to the employees or the employer. The officer cannot be held responsible for this collective bargaining negligence, since the parties must make up their own minds on the basis of whatever information they do or do not have.

When the meeting with the conciliation officer is held, it is customary for the officer to meet first with both parties together for the purpose of finding out what items are in dispute, to obtain the general views of both parties on the issues and where they think the bargaining is going. This kind of information is not provided to the officer in advance of the meeting since the application does not require any specifics about the bargaining or the issues other than the dates of the meetings and when notice to bargain was given, together with other general information such as the expiry date of the existing collective agreement, the number of employees in the bargaining unit and similar facts. It is crucial to the officer's purpose to define the boundaries of the dispute before attempts are made to conciliate, and only the parties can explain what is in dispute, or at least what each thinks is in dispute.

It is important for both respective spokespersons to be clear and precise in outlining the matters in dispute when the officer opens the meeting. One effective way to accomplish this is to prepare a written statement of what is in dispute, what respective proposals have been made and when these proposals were made, on each of the various matters. This document will not only assist the conciliation officer but it will be reviewed by the other party, and misunderstandings can be dealt with before negotiations advance further.

In outlining the matters in dispute, a spokesperson should be careful not to engage in rhetorical posturing or to argue at length the justification for a given position on a specific issue or issues. Before attempts are made to convince the conciliation officer of the merits of a position, the officer must first be told what the differences are between the parties. In short, this part of the conciliation meeting should be informative, not argumentative.

Once the parties have reviewed the matters in dispute with the conciliation officer, the usual practice is for the officer to separate the parties and for him or her to meet with one of the parties alone. At this stage, the officer will be probing to see whether the formal position of that party is rigid or flexible and also to get a feel for the bargaining goals and priorities of that party. The way in which an officer goes about this task depends largely on which party is involved and how willing the negotiators are to talk with candour. Speaking generally, the officer will question each committee as to its real (as distinct from stated) views on each of the matters, and may ask a number of questions, such as, do you really expect to get such and such a change from the other side, and how do you expect to get it to agree with you? The officer also tries to obtain the full confidence of each committee and to make the members feel he or she can help in reaching an acceptable settlement. The key here is that the officer has one single-minded purpose — to find a solution that both parties can accept. In the absence of agreement, the solution has no life and no existence.

It is imperative to remember that an officer can be of assistance only if the parties want help and are prepared to provide the officer with something to work with by way of compromise or flexibility on the issues. Put another way, either or both parties may determine that it is not in their interests to try to reach a settlement at this point in time. If this is the case, even the most skilled conciliation officer will be ineffectual. On the other hand, if the parties genuinely want to reach a collective agreement and are prepared to be frank with an officer, a settlement may be reached, even though the particular result may not have been acceptable in earlier direct negotiations.

A conciliation officer, to be effective, must obtain the confidence of both sides. Once the officer has determined that the parties are genuinely anxious to settle their differences, the negotiating landscape can be probed and explored to find common ground. It follows that the officer must be able to elicit how the parties actually feel about each issue, in contrast to how they have put forward their formal bargaining positions. Thus, the officer will push and pull to see what degree of movement the parties have, and to see whether the parties are going to continue to argue about matters that are not important to them. The point is that the officer will know only what the parties tell him or her, and they will talk only if they feel he or she can be trusted and wants to help them.

(d) Identification of issues

If there are a number of items in dispute and if the officer decides that the parties have not seriously discussed them or negotiated in a meaningful way, the parties may be directed to go away and meet on their own and report their bargaining progress to the officer. On the other hand, if the parties have had a number of discussions on each of the points that are still outstanding, the officer will want to know what is the factual basis, if any, for each party's position. The purpose of this exercise is not to impose any binding decision or to act like an arbitrator, but to decide if there is any collective bargaining logic in what is being said, and to consider whether the party is misinformed or mistaken in the information it is using. Similarly, if the bargaining response is an emotional reflex rather than an informed and thoughtful judgment, that will tell the officer more than he or she may want to know.

A detailed review in private of the points in dispute serves two other purposes. First, if a party has to explain its views on a given position to an outsider, this in itself may more accurately define the essence of the matter and, in some cases, a statement of the issue may suggest the answer. On occasion, the airing of a negotiating position itself resolves the matter, if only in the sense that the informing party becomes satisfied, as a result of the explanation and discussion, that a collective agreement change is unnecessary or unattainable. Secondly, the explanation allows the conciliation officer to judge whether the party feels strongly about the matter or whether it is merely performing a collective bargaining ritual — what is sometimes called a collective bargaining fan dance, an ornate combination of concealing, revealing and teasing!

Once the conciliation officer has reviewed the points in dispute with one party, he or she will normally proceed to have a similar discussion alone with the other party. At this stage the officer will not want to give any indication of the content of the discussions with the first party, or what areas of flexibility or compromise have been identified. What concerns the officer at this time are the overall intentions of the parties, and whether there seems to be a mutual and genuine desire to reach a settlement. If this intention exists, the officer can then turn to the specific items that must be resolved.

In the private discussions, the officer will be seeking direct answers to questions, particularly each party's willingness to change its bargaining stance and precisely how far. The spokespersons of the parties must recognize that the aim of the conciliation officer is to bring about a settlement, but not in the abstract; the parties must be willing to agree to specific realities. Understandably, the parties may be concerned as to how much information they should reveal to the conciliation officer, how open they should be in speaking to each of the specific proposals, and what they can or cannot do on each issue. The conciliation officer cannot be effective unless both parties are prepared to reveal their actual positions, as distinct from their formal negotiating positions. At the same time, the parties should advise the officer, in clear and specific terms, what information he or she is free to carry back to the other side and what information is for the officer's private use only.

One way to explain the point is in relation to the matter of wages. Assume that the employer has proposed a wage increase of 25¢ per hour per year to all employees in direct bargaining with the union, but is prepared to settle at a maximum increase of 50¢ per hour in order to reach agreement and avoid a strike. The employer spokesperson may be concerned that if the officer is given that figure, that is, 50¢ per hour, it may be revealed to the union bargaining committee by the officer prematurely, and will then be a new bargaining plateau. There are two ways to handle this problem. In one approach the employer spokesperson can state to the officer that the 25¢ per hour wage proposal is flexible and the employer is prepared to make an improvement by some unstated amount on that proposal. If the actual figure of 50¢ is not named, both the officer and the union bargaining committee can only speculate as to the precise degree of flexibility and how far beyond 25¢ the employer will go. The other approach is to name the figure but to tell the conciliation officer that it is for the officer's private information and is not to be conveyed to the other side without the employer's consent.

Once the matters in dispute have been identified and reviewed with both parties, the officer tries to narrow the specific differences and resolve the points in dispute. In some cases this requires either or both parties to make new proposals, apart from those tabled in the direct negotiations. In other instances, the officer makes suggestions to the parties by way of a compromise on a specific point, although the parties may ignore these initiatives from the officer. Since the conciliation officer is experienced and has nothing personal to gain, his or her ideas are really proposals from a neutral person. A major advantage of this approach is that the parties can accept the officer's suggestions, with whatever ill grace they feel is appropriate, without having to be seen to abandon a previously held bargaining position and consequent loss of face. In addition, if the idea turns sour, the negotiators have a common person to blame — the poor, hard-working officer, who was only trying to help!

As the meeting unfolds, the officer may conclude that there are simply too many matters in dispute to be resolved in one meeting. Thus, subsequent meetings may be scheduled with the officer, or the parties may be directed to meet on their own and to report their bargaining progress to the officer. As long as the officer detects a reasonable chance that a settlement will be reached, the conciliation efforts will continue, regardless of the number of meetings that must be held. During this time, it is to be remembered that no lawful strike or lock-out may take place.

Approximately one-half of the disputes that reach the conciliation officer stage are resolved at that level. In many cases a conciliation officer will find it impossible to effect a settlement, either because the parties are not prepared to bargain seriously or because the gap between them is unbridgeable. In the former situation, an experienced conciliation officer will quickly detect from what is said by the parties that, at this time, the conciliation results are not going to be fruitful. In the latter case, the officer may conduct a lengthy meeting or series of meetings before finally accepting the reality of an inevitable breakdown in negotiations.

(e) No-board report

If an officer concludes that a settlement cannot be reached, he or she prepares a report for the appropriate Minister. The report is an internal document and is a descriptive account of the state of the negotiations and includes the recommendations of the officer as to the appointment of a conciliation board or mediator, as the case may be. At least in theory, the Minister reviews the conciliation officer's report and determines whether or not to appoint a conciliation board. If a conciliation board is not appointed — and it will not be — a letter in the following terms is sent to the parties:

DATE

ABC Company Limited
123 Corporate Street
Toronto, Ontario

Dear Sirs:

Re: ABC Company Limited and Union Local 456

By direction of the Minister of Labour, The Honourable . . . . ,
I wish to inform you that after careful consideration he has decided not to appoint a board of conciliation in reference to the dispute between the above-mentioned employer and union.

Yours very truly,

per Deputy Minister

Fourteen days following the receipt of this letter, the employees may engage in a lawful strike and the employer may commence a lawful lock-out. Two days are allowed by statute for the service of this letter. As a consequence, the easiest way to calculate when a lawful strike or lock-out can take place is to count sixteen calendar days from the date that appears on the letter, including that day itself. The exception is in the case of the construction industry, where the equivalent time period is seven days rather than fourteen.

2. Boards of Conciliation

It has already been observed that, other than in the federal jurisdiction, conciliation boards are rare. There have, however, been occasions where a conciliation board has been appointed and it may be useful to make a brief comment on the subject.

A conciliation board is a three-person board, with one member appointed by each side and a chair either selected by the two nominees or appointed by the responsible Ministry. The primary purpose of the board is to conciliate, and the practices and techniques are much the same as those followed by a conciliation officer. One advantage of a three-person board is that each of the nominees can be expected to have the trust and confidence of the side that appointed him or her and, as a result, the chair can use the nominees to explore possible compromises or to look for any flexibility on the issues in dispute.

If the conciliation board is able to bring the parties together and reach a settlement, this ends its deliberations. On the other hand, if a settlement cannot be attained, a conciliation board, in contrast to a conciliation officer, may prepare and issue in writing formal recommendations to the parties as to a basis for settlement that in the board's view is appropriate. These recommendations, which are to both the parties and the Ministry of Labour, may be made public and, while not binding on the parties, would obviously be of persuasive value, depending in part on the stature and reputation of the persons on the board, the nature of the recommendations, especially where any public interest was affected, and the quality of the reasoning and analysis that caused the members of the board to conclude as they did. It is to be emphasized that a conciliation board would not be arbitrating a dispute and imposing terms but proposing a formula which, if adopted by the parties, would form the basis of the next collective agreement between them.

Chapter 7

Mediation

When a collective bargaining dispute has not been resolved at conciliation and the no-board report has been sent to the parties, the legal time-clock begins to run down to the date where a lawful strike or lock-out may take place. There is a fourteen-day interval from the issuance of the no-board report which gives the parties an opportunity to meet and negotiate before a lawful strike can commence. While the parties may meet and bargain on their own, another government mechanism, called mediation, has evolved which provides the disputing parties with assistance during those difficult and critical days.

During the 1950s and 1960s, boards of conciliation were frequently appointed following the breakdown of negotiations and after a conciliation officer had been unable to bring the parties together. While there is still provision for the appointment of a board in most labour relations Acts, it is rarely used, especially in the private sector. An exception is the federal jurisdiction, where conciliation boards are employed from time to time.

When boards of conciliation fell out of favour, a collective bargaining vacuum was created. As a consequence, some of the more inventive labour relations administrators designed a new role to be filled, and the conciliation officers assigned to this new role were called mediators. Effectively then, a third stage of bargaining has been added to direct bargaining and conciliation.

A mediator is like a conciliation officer with a different title who is performing a bridge-building function during a crisis bargaining situation. A mediator has no more power than a conciliation officer and no authority to require either party to do anything. A mediator, like a conciliation officer, must rely on being able to persuade the parties to reach their own collective agreement on whatever terms they find acceptable. The major difference is that a mediator meets with the parties in the days or hours immediately preceding a strike or lock-out and, if unsuccessful in averting the strike, continues to arrange meetings and maintain contact after the strike or lock-out has commenced. Thus, the mediator tries to effect a last minute settlement of a potential strike or lock-out, or tries to settle a strike or lock-out that has already begun.

There is no particular difficulty in obtaining the appointment of a mediator. There are no documents to complete or formal steps to follow. Either party may request a mediator or the Ministry of Labour may decide to appoint a mediator on its own initiative. The request may be in writing but can also be made in a telephone call. The request may be rejected, but this would be surprising unless the other side strongly objected. What is more likely is that the request will be deferred to give the parties more time to bargain on their own.

As a general rule, the mediator will be available to the parties as long as the dispute lasts. This is different in practice from the role of a conciliation officer, whose deliberations are ended once a report has been made to the Minister. A mediator may have a number of meetings with the parties extending over time while a strike or lock-out continues. In addition, efforts may have been made to keep the mediator's schedule free, so that meetings can be held on consecutive days to continue the momentum if negotiations are proceeding well or need additional time and attention. Like a good stew, negotiations may need to simmer for some time over a controlled heat for the full flavour to be released.

1. Role of the Mediator

The techniques used by a mediator are much the same as those used by a conciliation officer. Because of the looming strike date, however, the parties are likely to be more on edge, and the bargaining tension is likely to be greater. To some extent, a mediator will use the time pressure as a lever to persuade the parties to modify their positions. If a strike has not begun but the deadline is only a day or so away, that fact alone can be used by a mediator to force the pace of negotiations and to demand that hard bargaining choices be made. If a strike has already begun, a mediator will try to find some common ground to end the strike which is likely causing hardship and difficulties to the parties. The mediator forces the parties to come to grips with their own bargaining priorities and to accept responsibility for what is going to happen. The mediator does this by bringing the parties together and by saying to them, individually and collectively, "Your call!"

To some degree, the very existence of government bargaining procedures such as mediation and conciliation affects the bargaining strategies of both unions and employers. As a result, some parties do not bargain seriously until a strike or lock-out is imminent. Some unions believe that only then will an employer be under sufficient pressure to make the necessary concessions at the bargaining table, and these unions generally move through the early stages of bargaining as quickly as possible. By and large, if the parties have waited until the eleventh hour before starting serious talks, it is unlikely that a mediator will be useful or requested by the parties.

A mediator will frequently try to wear down the representatives of the parties, physically and mentally, by holding meetings that continue around the clock or in some cases even longer. A mediation meeting is an acknowledgment by both parties that a bargaining crisis is upon them. Although the dispute between them presumably results from strongly held views, the parties must also be aware that they have only a limited amount of time if a confrontation is to be averted. A mediator may therefore try to keep the parties in continuous discussions in the hope that one or both will break, or at least bend significantly, if only to get some rest.

Some critics of these marathon sessions have referred to them as virility contests. Male negotiators, especially macho types, revel in them. They can, however, be counter-productive because some individuals become overtired and make collective bargaining mistakes. In addition, the combination of weariness and tension is dangerous, and brings a different perspective to the issues as the meeting grinds on. On the other hand, a mediator may feel that the parties must be kept at work and forced to use all the available time continuously to find a resolution of their dispute. By continuing to press them to the limits of their energy, and by keeping the parties together, a mediator may find that a formula can be reached to bridge the gap before the negotiations — and the exhausted negotiators — collapse.

It may also be that the negotiating parties are not of one mind on all issues and priorities. Some members of the respective committees may be more or less militant than others. A mediator may therefore direct particular attention to those members of the committees who do not seem enthusiastically committed to an economic fight, and who may lead a movement towards settlement if only because they are unwilling to pay the high price of either having the meeting continue or having it break off without a settlement.

2. What Makes a Good Mediator?

The factors that make a good mediator are as difficult to describe as those that go to the selection of a spouse. There is no profile of the perfect mediator. Certain basic qualities are common to both conciliation officers and mediators. Indeed, a mediator can be described as a person who is trying to break up a fist-fight without getting slugged, while a conciliation officer attempts to dissuade the combatants from getting into a fight in the first place.

Perhaps the most important quality is the ability to obtain the trust and respect of the parties to a collective bargaining dispute. If the parties are not prepared to confide in a mediator and speak with candour, the mediator cannot act effectively. A mediator can be given the formal positions of the parties and the reasons why, in all righteousness, each is correct, but the parties will already have exchanged this information and neither has been convinced. What a mediator seeks out are the current positions, now that the dark days of potential conflict are here. How much will the employer give up to avoid a strike? What is the minimum the union must get? Is either of the parties presently committed to a strike? Does anyone care?

Like a conciliation officer, a mediator must be seen to have a high sense of integrity. If your position is flexible, you will not admit this to a mediator if there is any expectation that the information will be revealed to the other side without your consent or knowledge. Concepts like trust and integrity are abstractions, but they are nonetheless substantive qualities and, in a mediator, they are qualities that are essential. You may have difficulty explaining what they are, but you know intuitively if they are present or not.

In addition, a mediator, even more than a conciliation officer, must have an abundance of patience and tolerance. Some of the individuals with whom a mediator deals may be belligerent, obnoxious or simply difficult, and these qualities are exaggerated by the tension of conflict. The positions that either or both parties have taken may seem unreasonable or even outrageous. Nevertheless, the parties are entitled to their own views and to make their own decisions. Put another way, a mediator must find a way to persuade each party, which is represented by a committee made up of over-stressed and stretched persons, to come to a collective bargaining conclusion that will, in turn, be acceptable to another group of tired and fractious negotiators. Depending on the number of matters in dispute, the degree of difference between the parties on each of these items, and the human chemistry between members of the respective committees, this wearing-down process may take a large amount of time and a number of meetings with a mediator.

It has been suggested that a mediator must be tolerant. Another way to put this is to say that a mediator must be objective and avoid becoming emotionally involved in the collective bargaining dispute. It is likely that the parties have generated all the emotional heat that the dispute can stand — often more than is justified. The parties' own judgments may be clouded by this fact, and the objectivity and perception of a mediator may dissolve the rhetoric so that the parties can see for themselves how wrong they have been. What a mediator must also do is avoid being perceived by either party as being on one side or the other. This does not mean that a mediator cannot express a viewpoint with force and determination. However, if one of the parties forms a judgment, however mistaken or uninformed, that the mediator is not taking a neutral position between the parties but is acting as an advocate for the other side, the mediator's effectiveness will be lost.

A further quality required of a mediator is a finely tuned sense of collective bargaining timing. A mediator's sense of timing may be critical on each occasion a decision is made, particularly as the bargaining tension escalates and the mediation process unfolds — not necessarily as it should.

When should meetings be held, and at what time and place? When should one party's proposal be put to the other side? When should the parties be brought together in the same room for joint discussions, and when should private meetings take place, and with which persons? When should final positions be taken, and when should a mediator propose a possible compromise deal, and to which party, in which order, and on what terms?

3. Structure of Mediation Meetings

The mediator, when appointed, can prepare for the task ahead by reading and reviewing the report of the conciliation officer in the dispute. As a result, when the initial meeting takes place, the mediator will have some sense of the nature of the issues that were in dispute at conciliation, and what happened to those items. At the commencement of the first meeting, the normal procedure is to bring the parties together and for each to inform the mediator of what issues are still outstanding and the position of that party on each matter. The mediator will be listening and evaluating the representations being made by each of the respective spokespersons, and will be equally concerned with the manner and tone with which the comments are made and the attitudes and reactions of the members of both committees, in order to judge the current collective bargaining atmosphere and whether the people there are conciliatory or rigid. Thus, the mediator will proceed to deal with the views of the parties on two separate, but connected, levels. The first is a consideration of the merits of the arguments being advanced by both parties to justify their positions. The second level is to read and decipher the collective bargaining signals and messages from the parties to each other and to the mediator. The first asks the question "What?" The second asks "What does it mean?"

Once the opening presentations have been made, the mediator will likely separate the two parties and have private discussions with each of the committees in turn. Initially, the mediator will want to probe the views and feelings of the committees to gauge how strongly their positions are held. Again, it is not up to the mediator to decide whether a particular demand is meritorious. What the mediator wants to know is whether a position is being pushed seriously, or is being advanced for tactical reasons and can be traded off if the other side modifies a position in some other respect. For the negotiators, the purpose of this exercise is not to convince the mediator of the correctness of the position, but is intended to provide the mediator with ammunition and incentive to approach the other side to see if it can be persuaded to accept the first party's view of the matter. If the position can be sold, the mediator will want to know what that party needs, or thinks it needs, to back off on the issue.

In some situations, the mediator may detect that the parties are not nearly as far apart as it appears on the surface. After private discussions, the mediator may be convinced that the parties need a recommendation that will save collective bargaining face. This subject cannot be stressed too often. One of the parties may overstate its position and may find itself committed to a course of action on a given matter that allows no manoeuvring room, since it has put its case in extreme terms. As another example, one of the parties may have stated that it would never, ever, agree to a particular proposal. What may be required is a proposal or formula by the mediator that both parties can accept, so that the party that has impaled itself on its own all too rigid words can avoid having to reverse itself in an open way. For most of us, if we are going to be left with our pants down we want privacy, not a negotiating room with staring eyes and grinning mouths.

Two important observations should be made on this subject. The first is that the mediator will not normally make recommendations to the parties unless satisfied, from private consultations, that his or her recommendations will be accepted by them. The second point is that the recommendations of a mediator are not binding on either side in a legal sense. However, if one side accepts and the other does not, the rejecting party can be made to appear defensive, since the recommendation has come from a neutral person. For this reason, mediators traditionally approach the concept of making recommendations with caution, and then only after first exploring them with the parties and after they have indicated acceptance in advance.

While the mediator may prefer to meet with the full committees at all times, it is not uncommon for meetings to take place between one or two spokespersons for each side and the mediator. This is a particularly useful approach where the committees are large and fractious and where the spokespersons are experienced and responsible. Such meetings and discussions must be handled with care. Obviously, the dialogue between the individuals present can be more free-wheeling, as no one has to play to an audience that is not there. At the same time, it is imperative that the participants not reveal any of the content of the discussions, even to members of their own committees, unless the mediator allows them to do so or they feel compelled to do so because of the internal politics of their committee. If this is the case, they should tell the mediator and the other spokesperson what they intend to do and what they are going to say.

It is even more important that the spokespersons be careful in giving undertakings or commitments to either the mediator or to a representative of the other side. For example, if the mediator requests the view of one side as to whether a given proposal would be acceptable, no affirmative answer should be given (you should not answer "Yes!") unless the spokesperson is certain that the proposal will be agreed to by his or her own committee if it is offered. If not sure, the spokesperson should go and sound out the views of the committee on the matter, at the same time maintaining silence as to why the questions are being asked. It is of fundamental importance that whenever a spokesperson on either side states in a private discussion with the mediator, and especially if someone from the other side is present, that a certain position can be accepted, the person must be able to deliver on the commitment. If either the mediator or the other side feels they have been misled at any point, even on a minor matter, there will not only be antagonism but also a refusal to trust the words or deeds of the spokesperson and the party he or she represents. Absent trust there can be no meaningful discussion.

4. Sidebar Meetings

On occasion, one of the spokespersons may wish to talk to his or her counterpart alone, in order to explore privately a given matter. The same cautionary words apply to such discussion. In addition, the mediator — or conciliation officer if the parties are still at that stage — should be advised that the meeting is taking place, or will take place, and should also be told what happened and why. While the parties have the right to have a private meeting without informing anyone, including the mediator, there is a risk that the mediator or conciliation officer will inadvertently take some action that will conflict with the private arrangements that have been made.

An even broader principle must be considered in relation to these discussions. If a negotiator reneges on a promise or a commitment that has been given, the other negotiator will not only be angry, but will also regard the first negotiator as unworthy and a person who cannot be trusted. However, it is the party the negotiator represents that will pay the highest price. In the last analysis, the most important asset a negotiator has is personal reputation and integrity, and if this is lost, or even questioned, that person's effectiveness as a negotiator is greatly diminished. This does not mean that private discussions should be avoided, as in many cases the settlement of difficult disputes could not be attained without such meetings. Nor does it mean that there should not be an exchange of undertakings and commitments. What it does mean is that before a negotiator states an acceptance of a given position, or a willingness to modify a bargaining stance on a given matter, that spokesperson must be certain that the full committee will support the change or undertaking. Similarly, if a negotiator receives assurances from a person for the other side, and the commitment is subsequently broken, the negotiator should flatly refuse to have any further private dealings with that person, and should not be shy in explaining why.

5. Settlement of Strikes

In addition to trying to avoid strikes, a mediator frequently becomes involved in efforts to settle a strike that is already underway. The techniques for reaching a settlement of a strike are no different from negotiations that precede a strike, but certain new issues and obstacles may have arisen that create a different set of dynamics.

The first question that may arise is whether the parties may withdraw a previous offer and negotiate from a different position once a strike begins. In other words, are the parties bound by previous offers and counter-offers even though they have been rejected and a strike takes place? Can they start all over again? Subject to the general requirement to bargain in good faith, either or both parties may decide to take a different bargaining position and to change or vary positions on any of the items in dispute once a strike begins. Thus, a union may be prepared to settle on certain terms if a strike can be avoided, but the terms for settlement may be significantly higher after the beginning of a strike. Of course, while this is the legal position, there may be sound tactical reasons for leaving the past offers on the bargaining table, not the least of which is that a change by one party may trigger a countermove by the other.

Another issue that may become a pivotal position, depending on the length of the strike, is the duration of the collective agreement. This problem can surface in two ways. In the first place it may focus on the question of retroactivity on wage increases. Put simply, the issue here is whether an employee should be paid the full amount of the newly negotiated wage increase for all hours worked, back to the expiry date of the old collective agreement. If the interval between the expiry date of the old collective agreement and the settlement is short, the problem is not likely to be of critical importance. On the other hand, if negotiations have dragged on for a long period of time, the amount involved for each employee may be many hundreds of dollars, and the issue may have achieved a high profile and priority in direct relation to the escalating costs. It is to be stressed that the matter of retroactivity is a negotiable matter between the parties, and there is no statutory requirement that retroactivity in any form must be paid; it is up to the parties to negotiate their own deal. Even if retroactivity is negotiated and paid, it is usually payable to employees who were not only in the employer's employ on the date when the old collective agreement expired, but who are still in the employer's employ when the new collective agreement is ratified. New employees, that is, employees who were hired after the old collective agreement expired, would normally be paid retroactively on a *pro rata* basis.

The second way in which the issue of duration of a collective agreement can be considered deals with the specific expiry date of the new collective agreement. Again, if negotiations have carried on over a number of months and the old collective agreement has long since expired, a two-year agreement — if that is what the parties agree to — may in fact have one year and a couple of months to run from the day the new collective agreement is reached. Thus, the parties should be careful to specify whether the term of the new collective agreement is to run from the expiry date of the old agreement or from the date when the new collective agreement itself is reached. If the latter, is the effective date of the new collective agreement to be the date of ratification, the date of signing, or some other date?

Another issue that may complicate a strike situation and with which a mediator and the parties may have to deal is the question of replacement employees hired during the strike period. Is the employment of these persons — "scabs" in the union lexicon — to be terminated? If not, what is the status of the striking employees in view of their seniority rights, and what expectation do they have of when they will be returning to their jobs? Obviously, these are difficult and, in some cases, highly charged, emotional questions, since they deal with the rights that a striking employee has to keep his or her job.

A further issue that can arise concerns a situation where some form of violence has taken place during a strike and criminal charges have been laid, or some other form of legal proceedings initiated. One side may demand that all criminal charges and legal proceedings be dropped as a term of settlement of the collective agreement. The difficulty is that criminal proceedings, once instituted by the police, become part of the court procedures and cannot be withdrawn except with the consent of the local Crown Attorney. In most jurisdictions, a Crown Attorney will refuse to agree to a withdrawal of such charges, and may even consider that an agreement between the parties that requires outstanding criminal charges be dropped is in itself an interference with the administration of justice. Thus, the practice seems to have developed that neither the parties nor the mediator should treat criminal charges that have been laid and not yet heard as among the items that can be properly negotiated.

Very recently, the concept of preventive mediation (a quite different notion, since it takes place during the term of a collective agreement) has been introduced in some jurisdictions, notably in Ontario and in the federal jurisdiction. The foundation of this approach is that a government official meets with the parties, apart from and outside of the normal negotiating process, and while the collective agreement is operating, for the purpose of assisting them to improve their labour-management relationship. While there is obviously nothing to stop the parties themselves from accomplishing this on their own, there are occasions when a third party may be the creative catalyst that is needed and can give the parties guidance and assistance as a neutral. If the labour relations climate is improved and various flash-points are removed, it follows that the next set of negotiations between the same parties will be smoother and less contentious. What the program tries to do is simple: it gets the important union-management players together, with an agenda of identifying what their mutual problems are, how they can best be addressed, and by whom. It stresses the interpersonal relationships and contacts and what can be done to improve them, not in a theoretical sense but in actuality, by the individuals themselves.

Previously, mention was made of the ratification process, or how approval is given to a tentative agreement. Once the committees have reached a basis of agreement between them, the specific terms and provisions of the understanding are normally put into writing in the form of what is called a Memorandum of Settlement. The opening words of a Memorandum of Settlement would be to the effect that "The parties and the undersigned representatives of the parties unanimously agree to recommend to their respective principals the following as a complete settlement of all of the collective bargaining matters in dispute between them." The general terms of settlement would be set out, not necessarily with the full language for each new provision, but with enough information so that the substance or the basis of agreement on each item can be understood. Each party would then go to its principals and recommend the acceptance of the terms of the Memorandum of Settlement, the union to its membership and the employer negotiating team to a management committee or board of directors.

On the employer side there is no particular requirement about how this is done; it depends on the size and structure of the organization. On the union side a ratification vote will be governed by the union's constitution and by-laws. In some cases the vote is done by secret ballot, while in others it may be done by a simple show of hands at a meeting. In any event, the normal procedure is that the union arranges a meeting of the membership and a vote or other expression of opinion takes place on the proposed settlement. If the terms of settlement are ratified, the other side should be notified of this fact, preferably in writing. The complete collective agreement can then be prepared for the signature of the parties.

Chapter 8

Public Sector Collective Bargaining

While collective bargaining is alive and active in both the public and private sector, there are important differences both in the substance and mechanics of public sector collective bargaining. This chapter will focus on some of these differences.

The term "public sector employer" is used to denote an employer that provides services for a segment of the general public which controls, directs or funds, in some fashion, the policies and role of that employer. In some cases, the senior officers and officials of a public sector employer are selected by the community or appointed by elected representatives. The public sector employer's purpose for being is not to make a profit, or even to be held accountable for expenditures, but to give a service to the segment of the public that calls upon it. This is true even though some of the funds that the public sector employer receives may come from fees or charges for the services being performed.

In most cases, the public sector employer depends upon tax sources for at least part of its revenue. To this extent, the public sector employer is politically responsible and is held accountable, either directly or indirectly, to the taxpaying public that funds the revenue. The public sector employer may be a federal, provincial or municipal government, an agency of such government, an institutional body such as a hospital, an autonomous department of one branch of government such as a municipal police department, a commission or body that performs a particular kind of community service such as providing welfare benefits, and so on.

In some cases, the public sector employer will be governed for collective bargaining purposes by the provisions of the relevant labour relations Act, to the same degree and in the same way as most private sector employers. For example, the City of Calgary is an employer under the Alberta legislation, and no distinction is made between it and a private employer operating in the same city. In other cases, the employer may be governed for collective bargaining purposes by a separate statute, such as the *Police Act* or, in Ontario, the *Hospital Labour Disputes Arbitration Act*. In most provinces, the provincial government employees are governed by the provisions of a separate statutory labour relations code that determines the manner in which such employees may bargain collectively with their employer, limits or prohibits them from striking, and in some cases limits the matters that may properly be the subject of collective bargaining.

As an illustration, municipal governments perform a variety of services for a community which include the operation of parks and recreation areas, fire protection services and police services. The employees involved in park maintenance work, assuming they are employed in Ontario, are subject to the Ontario *Labour Relations Act* for collective bargaining purposes. The fire department employees of the same municipality are subject to the *Fire Departments Act*, and the police employees are subject to the *Police Act*. Thus, these three groups of employees are treated separately for collective bargaining purposes, even though they are all employed by the same municipal government. To extend the example, the employees of the local hospital or nursing home, while not employed directly by the municipal government, are covered by the *Hospital Labour Disputes Arbitration Act*.

The distinction that has been drawn has an important practical effect. If the employees in question fall within the scope of the relevant provincial labour relations Act, then, subject to any special treatment in the Act, they are entitled to go on strike in the event of a collective bargaining dispute with their employer in the same way as any employee of a private sector employer in the same jurisdiction. However, if the employees are not subject to the provincial labour relations Act but are covered by a separate statute, it may be that they are not entitled to go on strike, even if they are unable to reach a collective agreement with their employer. The usual method chosen for the resolution of such a collective bargaining dispute is compulsory binding arbitration, often called interest arbitration.

Consider the case of employees in the health care field. The registered nurses of a given Ontario hospital may obtain certification from the Ontario Labour Relations Board through their union, the Ontario Nurses Association. Once certified, the union meets with the employer and both parties are required to bargain in good faith with a view to entering into a collective agreement. In the event the parties are unable to reach an agreement, the nurses in the hospital are prohibited by the *Hospital Labour Disputes Arbitration Act* from going on strike, and the hospital in turn is prohibited from imposing a lawful lock-out on the nurses. Under the terms of the same Act, the union and the hospital may proceed to place the collective bargaining issues still in dispute between them before an arbitrator for a decision, which is binding upon all parties. Similarly, the provisions of the *Police Act* and the *Fire Departments Act* contain the same trade-off of the right to strike in return for the opportunity to have a third party decide the terms of the collective agreement, terms the employer must meet.

1. Effects of Compulsory Arbitration

If the particular employees may not lawfully go on strike at any time, the employer negotiators and the union representatives are faced with significant differences in the bargaining techniques they use and the pressures they can apply. To begin with, there is frequently a tendency for the public sector parties to avoid serious bargaining once they perceive arbitration to be inevitable, since the parties would not wish to prejudice their positions before an arbitrator. A party would not withdraw a particular proposal or make significant offers on the same matter or issue because, ultimately, the arbitrator is likely to make an award somewhere in between the positions of the parties at the time of the adjudication. In this sense, the parties, in early bargaining, may be more concerned with jockeying for an advantage in the arbitration process rather than trying to narrow or resolve issues at the bargaining table. To this degree, the imposition of arbitration may impede the candour and substance of the bargaining and, of course, if the parties view it as inevitable that they cannot themselves solve their bargaining problems, the prophecy becomes self-fulfilling.

A second way in which compulsory arbitration of collective bargaining disputes may affect bargaining strategy is to encourage either or both parties to abdicate the responsibility of resolving their own differences. Collective bargaining frequently requires the making of hard decisions that will bring criticism and dissent, and the acceptance of responsibility for those decisions. In some cases, an easy way out is to place the burden of making a controversial decision on an arbitrator, who in turn will receive whatever criticism may be levied, from whatever source. In that sense, a public sector negotiator has an easier time of it. If things go badly at the bargaining table, you can always run to an arbitrator. If you get what you want, you, as negotiator, can claim credit as a persuasive advocate. If not, you can blame the thick-headedness — or worse — of the arbitrator.

A further complicating factor is the political tension that surrounds any collective bargaining dispute in the public sector. From the employer's point of view, there is the need and obligation to provide a continuation of the services in question. At the same time, some of the employer negotiators who are elected persons may have to balance their own political considerations and priorities against the negotiating decisions that must be made. The elected officer, for example a school board trustee, wants to be re-elected. At the same time, the trustee is necessarily aware that to agree to certain kinds of economic demands will bring about significant tax increases, an issue that same trustee is already on the political record as opposing. The push and pull of the political conflict imposes an obvious strain on the analysis of the collective bargaining issues the trustee is considering in balancing his or her public responsibilities and his or her private, political interests.

Unfortunately, but inevitably, the merits and values of the two worlds are seldom the same, and often collide.

From the union side, the union representatives have a responsibility to the union members to obtain the best possible terms and conditions of employment in the collective agreement that is being negotiated. If they are prohibited by law from engaging in a lawful strike, they may only obtain their collective bargaining objectives by one of two means. On the one hand, they can endeavour to persuade the employer negotiators, let us say the elected town officials, to agree to the increases in wages and other benefits that they seek. If they cannot attain this result, they can follow the second route, namely, to try and persuade an arbitrator to grant the increases they want in an arbitration award. However, the union representatives and members are all part of the same community that must finance such increases if awarded by an arbitrator. It will be seen that the negotiators of both sides in a public sector bargaining situation not only have to be concerned with the positions and postures of the other party, but, in contrast to the private sector, they can be influenced by the conflicts between their own self-interest and their responsibilities to the public in the community. The extent of the conflict, or even whether a conflict is perceived, depends on the individual. If the dispute proceeds to arbitration, the arbitrator is, or should be, concerned with the same conflict and tension caused by the dynamics of private interests rubbing against public responsibilities.

Most public sector employers, and those unions that bargain with them, are aware of these special considerations. In the last analysis, the collective bargaining process is adversarial in nature, but the objective of the process is to reach mutually satisfactory terms of agreement and to avoid economic confrontations. In the result, different techniques have been developed which have enabled the parties in the public sector to deal better with their own collective bargaining disputes.

Many public sector employers have administrative staffs to handle the day-to-day business affairs, while the political decisions are made by elected officials. For instance, the mayor and council of a municipal government make policy, but do not themselves administer the ongoing operations of the municipal corporation. These tasks are carried out by the employees of the municipal government, in accordance with the policy directions established for them by the elected representatives.

In order to avoid some of the problems that have been already referred to, many elected officials prefer to leave the conduct of the actual collective bargaining to administrative officials, subject to policy guidelines established for the negotiators. In this way, the actual bargaining is done by management employees of the public sector employer within the negotiating framework established for them, and the resulting settlement, once attained, is subject to ratification by the elected officials. This approach may be useful for the employer, but the union, to counter it, may wish to go over the heads of the administrative persons assigned by the employer to do the bargaining, and make a presentation directly to the elected officials, preferably in a public hearing. Few politicians wish to be faced in an open meeting with the provocative questioning and the need to take forceful positions on real issues that are part of collective bargaining. The employer negotiators will often seek to keep elected officials out of the bargaining process, and the union will try to involve them so as to exploit the irresistible temptation of elected people to comment on things they know nothing about, or to do things that may make sense politically but are less than helpful to the negotiators. For example, politicians talk, often far too much. Negotiators, in contrast, have to spend at least equal time listening.

2. Source of Funds

A further dimension that complicates the bargaining concerns a matter of eternal interest to all of us — money. The operating funds of a public sector employer may come from a number of sources including different layers of government. In the health care field, the majority of the funds available to a local hospital do not come primarily from the community it serves but from the provincial Ministry of Health and, less directly, from the federal government. When certification is granted, a union is certified as the collective bargaining agent for the employees of that particular hospital. The union may be told by the hospital with which it is bargaining that there are no funds available to pay the increases being sought, or that the provincial funds allocated to the hospital to pay future wage increases cannot be more than a given percentage in excess of the preceding year's budget. In reality, it is the Ministry of Health that determines the amount of money available to the hospital, rather than officials or representatives of the hospital. The ghost that hovers over the bargaining table is the Ministry of Health, but the only direct participants in the bargaining are the hospital negotiators and the bargaining committee of the union. Thus, the body that can grant the wage increases the union wants is not there to be persuaded or entreated. Simply put, the employer negotiators at the bargaining table are sheltered and insulated, but the union representatives are frustrated.

There have been efforts made to rationalize the effect of some of these difficulties, and to put the principal actors together on the same stage. Bargaining may take place between a number of public sector employers, in the same industry or geographical area, and the same union, or joint bargaining may take place between a number of employers and a number of unions or locals of the same union. The bargaining, therefore, may be regional in nature, or it may even be province-wide. It cannot be said that any of these attempts is a complete answer. The real problem is that the collective process may be subject to demands that it cannot handle, such as expecting people to bargain when the important decision makers are not present, or expecting that, through bargaining, what is regarded as inadequate funding or wrong fiscal priorities can be corrected or reversed. The bargaining process can accomplish much, but it has its limitations in dealing with issues that are treatable only through institutional or societal action, on a scale and at a level far removed from the direct parties to the bargaining.

Apart from the considerations that have been mentioned, the parties to the public sector dispute conduct their bargaining, in the technical or mechanical sense, in the same manner as if they were involved in the private sector. Of course, this is so only up to the point where the unresolved matters in dispute are taken to compulsory arbitration under the appropriate legislation, where a lawful strike or lock-out is statutorily prohibited. While the topic of interest arbitrations is not, strictly speaking, the subject of this book, it should not be left without some comment.

3. Interest Arbitration

Broadly speaking, there are two categories of arbitration cases handled by Canadian arbitrators. The first is called a rights arbitration, which involves the interpretation, application, or alleged violation of a provision of an existing collective agreement. The second is known as an interest arbitration, and involves the creation and imposition of the terms of a collective agreement on the parties to such agreement. The arbitrator fills in the gaps in the collective agreement that the parties could not complete for themselves.

Under the statutes that have been referred to which establish an interest arbitration, the matters in dispute are presented, in most cases, to a three-person arbitration board. Each party selects its own member, and these two persons then choose a third person to act as chair of the arbitration panel or board. If they are unable to make a choice, the chair is appointed for them by the appropriate Minister in the province. The arbitration board convenes a hearing, and the parties are invited to present to the arbitrators their submissions on the issues referred to the board for disposition. The board is required to make a decision on each of the matters referred to it, in the sense that the board has to make a determination as to whether the collective agreement should or should not include the provision that is being arbitrated. The terms of the award of the board of arbitration are final and binding upon the parties and, in the normal course of events, cannot be the subject of an appeal to the courts, unless there has been a significant error of law or a refusal to allow a party to the proceedings to present its case and the evidence in support of its position.

The general practice for each party appearing before an arbitration board is to make its presentation in a written brief which can be supplemented by additional oral arguments and representations. Much of the information before a board of arbitration would be in the nature of comparative data and material on the matters in dispute that are being considered. For example, if one of the points in dispute is wages, the parties would table information of a statistical nature, comparing what other arbitrators have done, what other employers are paying their employees in the same industry, the wages in similar industries in the same geographical area or outside the area — in short, a detailed and documented rationale, on a comparative basis, to enable the arbitrator to make an informed and, depending on which side is presenting the data, an enlightened decision.

Unless the parties have otherwise agreed, the arbitrator has full authority to make a decision that does not result in awarding the position of either party, but is somewhere between their respective submissions or outside the range of the options they have provided. On occasion, the parties may choose what is called the final offer selection method, in which event the arbitrator's jurisdiction is limited to choosing the position of one of the two parties. Under the final offer selection method, the arbitrator must find that he or she prefers the position of either the employer or the union. For instance, if the employer's position on wages is 4% and the union's position is 8%, the arbitrator could award either 4% or 8% but could not award 6%. It is to be emphasized that the arbitrator's powers would not be limited in this way unless the parties had first agreed that the arbitrator must follow the final offer selection method.

While each interest arbitration award turns on the issues involved and the merits of the submissions of the parties on those issues, arbitrators have tried to set out some principles of general application. One major consideration, that seems to be universally adopted by interest arbitrators, is that public sector employees should not be required to subsidize the community by accepting inferior wages and working conditions. On the other hand, the invocation of this principle requires the arbitrator to make comparisons in order to ensure that the wages and working conditions are not substandard, either by comparison with employees employed elsewhere in the same industry or on the basis of comparisons in the specific community.

Arbitrators have grappled with the concept of equity as applied to interest arbitrations. It has been recognized that the best comparison is with collective agreements which have been freely negotiated in the same area and industry. Therefore, community compensation standards, established through the exercise of collective bargaining, are given substantial weight. On the other side, equity as a general standard must be applied not only to the parties, but to the taxpaying public which is the ultimate source of the funds. The majority of taxpayers have the right to engage in collective bargaining to obtain their own compensation rights and conditions. The employees who are the subject of the arbitrator's consideration have had their rights curtailed by the legislature, as essential service employees who may not engage in strike action at any time. Thus, the public, through the legislature, has determined that an uninterrupted service must be provided by the employees, but, correspondingly, the same public must be prepared to pay those who provide the services, wages and benefits that are commensurate with community standards.

The external criteria would involve the arbitrator examining the rates of pay or other conditions of employment in effect elsewhere in the province, or outside the province, where similar employers exist. Of lesser importance, but certainly relevant, would be whether the other communities being surveyed were of a similar size, and whether the tax base was comparable. Similarly, the arbitrator would be expected to examine other interest arbitration awards, particularly in the same industry. The local criteria are more difficult to enunciate. Fire department employees in one municipality can be easily compared, as to their terms of employment, with other fire department employees in other municipalities. It is significantly more difficult to look at the same community, find comparable jobs within the community, and then compare those against the position of firefighter. Carrying the same example one step further, one can evaluate the position of a police officer in relation to a firefighter in the same municipality even though the jobs are by no means identical. It is not as easy to compare the same firefighter with other municipal employees in the same community who are performing other tasks, such as working in the parks, because the jobs are so different as to make the comparisons largely invalid. Despite these difficulties, arbitrators have considered the terms of agreement of employees who have bargained collectively and reached agreement with their municipal employer as a factor in their deliberations. The weight to be given to that factor depends on how close are the comparables. In short, the results of collective bargaining will provide a focus for the arbitrator and a scale of comparables to give the award balance and credibility in the community.

One area of public sector collective bargaining should be the subject of special mention. In Ontario, school teachers in both the secondary and primary schools are governed by the *School Boards and Teachers Collective Negotiations Act*. This statute was enacted in 1974 and contains a number of collective bargaining innovations, some of which have proved effective in some circumstances. For instance, under the Act, a fact-finder may be appointed, who meets with the parties for the purpose of rationalizing and evaluating the issues between them. The fact-finder may issue a written report, which includes his or her views on what would be a proper resolution of the particular matter. The report is not binding on the parties, but it does inform the public about the nature of the dispute and what may be a reasonable solution to it. The fact-finder's report may also be helpful in providing a focus or direction to the parties in their subsequent bargaining on the same issue or issues.

One of the significant difficulties facing negotiators in the public sector, especially on the management side, is a lack of information on comparative rates and conditions of employment. To some degree this is understandable, since the public sector employer is primarily concerned with its own operations, but the fact remains that there is often an inadequate sharing of cost information among employers. Some negotiators are of the view that an easily accessible data information bank should be established for the purpose of enabling employer and union negotiators to obtain accurate cost comparisons for negotiating purposes. This is a concept that is both useful and needed.

4. Importance of Public Sector Bargaining

It is self-evident that public sector collective bargaining affects all of us. If the bargaining breaks down and a strike takes place, important or even essential services are denied to the community. If the strike is unlawful, not only are the services in question not performed, but law enforcement agencies become involved, with a further polarization of both the parties and the public, and with the media yelling and snapping from the sidelines. In that sense, a public sector collective bargaining confrontation raises higher public emotions than all but a very few private sector situations.

It may be argued that collective bargaining, as we know it in North America, should not apply to the public sector in Ontario. The fact is that the right to organize and bargain collectively has been granted to most employees in the public sector, and therefore the debate should not deal with the merits of whether collective bargaining should be granted, but rather should centre on an analysis of how to make such bargaining work better.

Some of the ways in which this can be accomplished have already been touched upon. There must be a greater recognition of the significance of the funding of public sector employees, and the need to have the funding agencies participate in the bargaining. Ghosts should not control the bargaining, but representatives of the real and actual decision makers should sit at the bargaining table, or at least be accountable to the negotiators. In some areas, both the employers and the unions should be prepared to accept that separation often means divisiveness, and should engage in meaningful joint bargaining and avoid jurisdictional quarrels that stem from an over-reliance on local autonomy. Two obvious examples are the health care field and school boards. There should be a means of providing specific and detailed comparative data to both sides while bargaining is taking place, and on which all parties can rely. At present, there is no neutral statistical agency, apart from the education field, where interested parties can obtain reliable and up-to-date information to assist them in their bargaining, although some employer groups and unions have put together information banks for their own use. Finally, there should be more attempts to innovate mechanisms that are appropriate to the special dynamics of the public sector bargaining scene. Conciliation boards may on occasion be of value, particularly where recommendations with reasons are issued by the board if a settlement is not reached. Similarly, it may be advisable to erect a public service tribunal with wide-ranging authority to order recalcitrant parties to bargain further, to appoint a fact-finder, to permit a selective strike of certain groups, to direct what parties should be at the bargaining table and on what terms, and, in short, to employ a full range of labour relations and bargaining options, with or without appropriate sanctions, so as to make public sector bargaining work. Since the premise that underlies private sector bargaining — the use of economic actions — does not apply for the most part in the public sector, it follows that a different set of bargaining techniques should be used, and it is surely not beyond our capacity to develop them.

However, there should be no illusions; the suggestions that have been made are more in the nature of bandaids on the process. They do not resolve the dilemma which is central to the difference between public and private sector bargaining. This essentially is the distortion of the use of mutual and offsetting powers and sanctions that must exist, if only in a rough sense, for collective bargaining to function. In a private sector employer situation, the confrontation, if it comes to that, is between the employer, the union and the employees. Unless the employer is the dominant economic power in the community, no direct economic pressures are brought to bear on the public. The parties can slug away at each other, literally and metaphorically, but the public is not involved. In a public employer strike or lock-out, the public necessarily becomes directly involved, in that the services that were being provided and for which it has paid its tax dollars are removed. Thus, one of the parties uses an economic club on an outside party, the public, in the hopes that the resulting pain and outrage will result in generating pressure for settlement.

The point ought not to be obscured by rhetoric. When the school teachers go on strike, or the school board locks them out, the action is taken with the hope and expectation that the parents of the affected students will demand an immediate cessation of hostilities and a re-opening of the school. Put bluntly, the educational future of the students is held up to ransom as part of a deliberate collective bargaining strategy.

These observations are not meant to be critical of either side. The difficulty is that the concept and principles of collective bargaining were originated in the private sector and then imported into the public sector. The public sector collective bargaining scene has become strained because, instead of two parties doing the bargaining and accepting the consequences of any confrontation, three parties are involved. However, only two parties do the actual collective bargaining, and the other, the public, pays the major price of either a settlement or a strike. Since the public is dragged into the dispute as a reluctant participant only after the economic fight begins, and since the public has as much or more to lose than the parties, the public interest should be more adequately protected at each stage of the bargaining process. In addition, public sector negotiators can learn much from their fellow negotiators in the private sector about how to manage the bargaining process more effectively and efficiently and how to be better bargainers.

Chapter 9

Bargaining Language Issues

1. Preamble

This part of the book deals with an explanation and analysis of some of the most common terms of any collective agreement, without differentiating between different kinds or scale of businesses. In order to make the discussion of value, I felt it necessary not only to comment on each subject-matter in general terms, but also to provide illustrations and examples of actual clauses. It must be understood that these examples are not provided as models of perfect drafting that you should use in your own collective agreement. To the contrary, in a number of cases the wording is clumsy and opaque. However, each clause and article that is reproduced comes from an existing collective agreement, and represents the offspring of a living, breathing, collective bargaining relationship. As in the medical field, an examination of a real body, with all its warts and imperfections, teaches more than a series of stylized anatomical sketches in a textbook.

The drafting of the perfect collective agreement — one that will provide a clear and acceptable answer to every conceivable employment situation — is an elusive concept. Still we can try, and we should. The following pages may help to give you not only a better understanding of concepts and the options that underlie the provisions common to most collective agreements, but also a sense of direction as to how the negotiating ideas can be better expressed in written form, by reviewing the way some parties have expressed their own collective agreements, for better or for worse.

As we have seen, collective bargaining issues are traditionally divided into non-economic, or language issues, and economic issues. The latter can be costed in more or less precise terms, and the total of the dollar impact of each of the economic provisions of a collective agreement, added together, will be the direct economic cost of the resulting settlement. I want to repeat, the language issues may have enormous consequences to the parties and, in some cases, these consequences have far greater impact on the viability of the operations than the direct economic issues. Employers ignore language issues at their peril.

To put the matter in focus, an employer is frequently concerned with its freedom to manage the business and to operate without the need to consult with the union that represents its employees, either when a management decision is made or in its implementation. Thus, an employer may wish to be contractually free to utilize any source of labour that it chooses in the contracting out of work, to transfer and lay off employees without special regard to seniority, and generally to operate and manage its business in whatever way it wishes, without interference from anyone, especially a union. The union, in contrast, recognizes that the employer's decisions made in these areas can result in employees being directly affected, either in their earnings or, in some cases, in their employment. As a result, the union has the right, and from its point of view the responsibility, to insist on protecting the rights and interests of such employees, either by restricting the employer's right to manage or by becoming involved in the decision of what is to be done, and when and how it is to be implemented. Therefore, the parties would be trying to reach an accommodation of these respective interests and concerns at the bargaining table, and to strike a balance that both can live with, at least for this point in time.

If the parties are dealing with the renewal of a collective agreement, they are bargaining on amendments or additions to the existing contractual language. If they are bargaining for a first collective agreement, they are starting, literally, with a blank piece of paper and writing down the structure and wording of a collective agreement from scratch. While the parties to any particular collective agreement may deal with a great number of collective bargaining language issues, the following chapters contain a discussion of some of the more common topics and examples of particular provisions.

2. Names of Parties

It may seem self-evident that the parties to a collective agreement must be identified by name. The issue is, what name? Occasions arise where a national or international union is the certified bargaining agent, but a bargaining proposal is made for the local union to be named as one of the parties. Sometimes, the proposal is that both the international and the local be named. There is no legal restriction to prevent the parties from naming the local union as a party to the collective agreement, notwithstanding the fact that the international union, rather than the local, was granted certification. It could be argued that in doing so the employer has recognized a different union from the union that was certified, since labour relations boards make a distinction between the international union and a local union of the same international, and consider them as separate entities.

This distinction is more a matter of theoretical than practical concern in most cases. However, one consideration that an employer should weigh in agreeing to the local union being identified as a party to the collective agreement, rather than the international, is the difficulty in recovering damages on an award by an arbitrator in the event that the union is found to be in breach of its obligations under the collective agreement. Such an event may arise where an unlawful strike takes place and the employer files a grievance under the collective agreement to claim compensation for the damage caused by the unlawful strike. The local union treasury may be inadequate to enable the employer to recover the amount of compensation awarded by an arbitrator. For this reason, as well as to avoid any argument as to whether the employer has recognized a different union than that certified, the preferable practice from the employer's point of view is to name in the collective agreement the same union that was certified.

One further difficulty can arise in respect of the naming of a local union as a party to the collective agreement. Some unions create composite locals, where the local union is comprised of members who are employees of more than one employer's operation and more than one bargaining unit. Thus, a particular local union may deal with several employers, perhaps in the same industry, although not always, and its membership will be made up of employees from these various employers. This may create difficulties for any particular employer, since the representatives of the composite local union, as well as the membership, will have concerns beyond that individual employer and may tailor their bargaining strategy to meet those interests. For example, if a tentative agreement is reached, who is to ratify the agreement? Should it be all members of the local union, only some of whom are members of the bargaining unit and directly governed by the new collective agreement?

From the union point of view, it is important that the actual employer of the employees in the bargaining unit is named as a party to the collective agreement, and if there is more than one employer, to have all the employers made parties. If certification has been granted to the union with respect to more than one employer, and joint negotiations take place which result in one master collective agreement, the agreement should identify each separate employer that is a party. To avoid disputes and confusion, the usual practice is to identify the employer by using the same corporate name as is set out in the certification order.

3. Purpose

Many collective agreements begin with an opening article which may be entitled "purpose", or in some cases "preamble". The idea behind this provision is to describe in broad and sweeping terms the joint or shared objectives that the parties have provided in detail in the provisions of the collective agreement that follows. The article does not set out specific rights or obligations of either party but, quite literally, describes the purpose of entering into the collective agreement and how the parties intend to conduct their collective agreement business together during the agreement's term. In that sense, the purpose article is a "hope" clause, sometimes pious, as it sets out no specific rights or obligations, but it can be used to give shape and colour to the interpretation of another provision of the collective agreement if a dispute arises as to that provision's meaning or application. It should be understood that there is no requirement, by statute or otherwise, that the parties agree on a purpose article, but many parties to collective agreements have felt it appropriate to include in their agreement such an article.

Two examples of a purpose article are as follows:

Example 1

The general purpose of this agreement is to establish mutually satisfactory relations between the company and its employees; to establish and maintain satisfactory benefits, working conditions, hours of work, and rates of pay; and to record the procedure for the prompt and equitable disposition of grievances for all employees who are subject to the provisions of this agreement.

Recognizing the common dependence of the company and of its employees upon the success of the business as a whole, the parties to this agreement support the mutual objective of increased productivity and efficiency, and jointly promote the goodwill between the parties that is necessary to the achievement of this objective.

Example 2

It is the purpose of this agreement to promote and improve relations between the employer and those of its employees who are represented by the union, and to set forth the terms and conditions of employment of such employees, and to deal with the relationship concerning other matters as between the parties hereto.

4. Recognition

This topic has already been dealt with in a previous chapter, at least to some extent. It will be recalled that agreement on a recognition article is required by statute. The purpose of the recognition article is to identify the bargaining unit for which the union is the bargaining agent, and thereby identify the employees who are subject to and covered by the terms of the collective agreement. Conversely, the positions that are expressly agreed by the parties to be excluded from the application of the collective agreement and which are outside the scope of the bargaining unit must also be listed and spelled out. For instance, forepersons are normally excluded from an industrial bargaining unit, both in the wording of the certification order and by the application of the recognition article in the resulting collective agreement.

Whatever words are chosen for the recognition article, it is imperative that the parties be clear and precise as to who is covered and who is not. As stated, the most common practice is to word the recognition article in the same terms as the certification order. Once the terms of the recognition article have been agreed upon, it is not uncommon to insert in the collective agreement a further clause, to make it clear that the persons described in the bargaining unit are the employees for the purposes of the application of the collective agreement. For example, such a clause may read as follows:

"Employee" as used in this agreement shall mean those persons described in the bargaining unit set forth in clause .01.

Some collective agreements provide in the recognition clause that the union is the bargaining agent on behalf of all of the employees whose classifications or job titles are set out elsewhere in the collective agreement or who perform certain kinds of job functions, such as a particular trade or craft. This form of wording is not to be regarded as sound practice, since there may be difficulties in dealing with new jobs or different jobs that are established after the collective agreement has been executed. For this reason, it is preferable to describe the boundaries of the bargaining unit within the framework of the recognition article and then, if necessary, to deal with the matter of job titles or classifications in some other part of the collective agreement.

5. Management Rights

From an employer's perspective, the management rights provision may be the most fundamental and critical part of the collective agreement. The purpose of this article is to set out in contractual terms what limitations have been agreed upon in the decision making by the employer as to the way and manner in which the business or operation will function, and what role, if any, the union and the employees will play in both the making of decisions and the results.

Most employers want freedom to operate the business and manage the affairs of the operation without an obligation to consult the union or to provide an opportunity to the union to vary or change a decision of management. From the union point of view many, if not most, management decisions touch the working lives of the members of the bargaining unit and have an impact on all persons that the union represents. Consequently, the union has a need to limit the right of management to make unilateral decisions and to restrict the employer from making decisions that cannot be questioned. The result is a direct confrontation between the negotiating principals. The employer demands a management rights article giving it broad and sweeping authority to operate the business. The union, on the other hand, wants to erect restrictions on the exclusive right of management to make decisions that could affect the interests of the employees in the bargaining unit. The specific kind of restriction could range from a requirement on the employer to consult with the union prior to a decision being made, a provision giving the union the right to grieve particular management decisions that appear contrary to specified criteria, or, in some cases, a prohibition on the right of management to take specific action, such as contracting out work, or, if the action is taken, a requirement to protect the jobs of existing employees.

The generally accepted arbitration theory is that management has the right to make decisions, even where such decisions affect employees covered by the bargaining unit, provided there is no contractual restriction on either the making or the implementation of the decision itself. Thus, to illustrate, provided there is no provision concerning the scheduling of work in the collective agreement, and even though there is no mention of that subject in the management rights article, the employer is free to schedule work at its sole discretion since this is a normal and customary right of management. However, most employers and unions prefer to define in their collective agreement the specific areas within which management has the right to make its own decisions. At least this may help to avoid disputes while the collective agreement is still operating. Thus the practice has developed, particularly in the private sector, for the management rights article to have a broad and general introductory paragraph, followed by subparagraphs that set out the individual areas within which management may make decisions, with or without restrictions. While there are many variations in collective agreements in the wording of a management rights article, three examples are set out below:

Example 1

The union recognizes and acknowledges that the management of the plant and direction of the working force are fixed exclusively in the employer and, without restricting the generality of the foregoing, the union acknowledges that it is the exclusive function of the employer to:

(a) **maintain order and efficiency;**

(b) **hire, promote, demote, classify, transfer, suspend and rehire employees, and to discipline or discharge any employee with seniority for just cause provided that a claim by an employee who has acquired seniority that he or she has been discharged or disciplined without** just cause may be the subject of a grievance and dealt with as hereinafter provided;

(c) make, enforce and alter, from time to time, rules and regulations to be observed by the employees;

(d) determine the nature and kind of business conducted by the employer, the kinds and locations of plants, equipment and materials to be used, the control of materials and parts, the methods and techniques of work, the content of jobs, the schedules of production, the number of employees to be employed, the extension, limitations, curtailment or cessation of operations or any part thereof, and to determine and exercise all other functions and prerogatives which shall remain solely with the employer.

Example 2

The company has the exclusive right and power to manage its operations in all respects and in accordance with its commitments and responsibilities to the public, to conduct its business efficiently and to direct the working forces and, without limiting the generality of the foregoing, it has the exclusive right and power to hire, promote, transfer, demote or lay off employees, and to suspend, discharge or otherwise discipline employees. The company agrees that any exercise of these rights and powers shall not contravene the provisions of this agreement.

Example 3

Subject to the provisions of this agreement, the management and the operation of the plant and the direction of the working forces is and shall remain vested exclusively in the employer. The employer retains all rights and privileges which are not specifically relinquished by the present agreement.

As a general protective and restrictive override, the union may add a further clause providing that in the exercise of the management functions already set out in the article:

The employer agrees that these functions will be exercised in a manner consistent with the provisions of this agreement.

The addition of such a clause makes it clear that the actions or decisions of the employer, including those matters set out in the preceding words of the article, cannot cancel or diminish specific contractual rights that have been given to the union and the employees elsewhere in the collective agreement. To put the point another way, the employer cannot shelter behind either the general or the specific wording of the management rights article and ignore another provision in the collective agreement where the parties have agreed that kind of management decision may only be applied in certain circumstances. For example, while the employer may have the right to decide on the number of employees to be used on a particular operation and to initiate a lay-off because of work requirements, such lay-off, and the actual persons to be laid off, would be determined by the application of the seniority article in the collective agreement. Thus, the right of the employer to decide on the total number of employees to be employed in the business at any one time is derived from the management rights article, but the method of deciding which employees will remain at work and who will be laid off is decided by the particular formula in the seniority article.

Another variation concerns the question of plant rules and regulations. Many collective agreements provide that management has the right to enact, alter and enforce rules and regulations, but that the alteration of existing rules should be a matter of discussion and consultation or, in some cases, agreement with representatives of the union. The following is an expression of this approach:

... but before altering any such rules the employer will discuss same with the union grievance committee and give them an opportunity of making representations with regard to such proposed alterations.

Obviously, the terms of the management rights article must reflect the particular kind of operation that is the subject of the collective agreement. The examples that have been provided are taken from private sector collective agreements, and parties in the public sector may want to reword some of this language to reflect the different climate in which some public sector managers operate. However, in the light of some of the more recent economic difficulties that affect all parts of the labour relations community, the differences between the public and private sectors in operating their respective businesses have been blurred, and the requirement for clear and expressive language for employers, unions and employees in all sectors has become more important. In past years, lay-offs were unheard of in many areas of the public sector, but now job security is as vital there as in the private sector. As a result, most public sector employers and unions recognize that a collective agreement, in particular the management rights provision, has to be evaluated against that mutual concern. Similarly, some public sector employers have examined the concept of contracting out as a means to cut costs and make certain operations more efficient. This, in turn, causes public sector unions to try to protect their members by insisting on wording in the collective agreement to prohibit such management actions. If agreement cannot be obtained, the union may try to negotiate language that in some way modifies the right of the employer to contract out work being done by employees in the bargaining unit.

The protection that is negotiated may be a simple assertion that the employer may not contract out work that normally is performed by employees in the bargaining unit. A more flexible provision would provide that contracting out may take place where certain situations arise, such as where the employer does not have sufficient employees available with the necessary skills to perform the work. Another approach is to provide that the employer may contract out work provided that, as a result, none of the existing employees are laid off or have their hours of work reduced.

If the collective agreement is to provide that no work normally done by employees in the bargaining unit may be contracted out to another employer under any circumstances, the wording should be direct and unambiguous. If, on the other hand, the parties have agreed to a different arrangement, the wording should be clear as to precisely what the parties have agreed to. For example, it may be that the parties agree that management may contract out work normally done by employees in the bargaining unit "provided that as a direct result no employees in the bargaining unit are laid off". These words seem to be clear enough. But suppose the collective agreement provides that management has the right to contract out work "only if such work may be performed by another employer in a more economically advantageous way to the first employer". These words invite argument because they are fuzzy. The difficulty with trying to find exact language to express broad concepts is that it may create as many questions as it answers. As another example, consider that some collective agreements provide that the employer, before contracting out work, must first consult with the union. But precisely what does the word "consult" mean? What is the meaning of such language if the union, once consulted, disagrees with the decision of management to enter into the contract? Does the obligation to consult mean to agree? Or, again, is a letter written by a plant manager to a local union president informing him or her of a decision "consultation"?

The point to make is that in drafting language for a collective agreement, the greater the precision and clarity of the words by which the parties set out what they have agreed to, the easier it will be for the parties to the collective agreement and any persons that are affected by its operation to understand what the agreement says. If they understand, it is less likely they will be in dispute.

A further subject that may arise during any analysis of management rights involves restrictions on the work that can be assigned to non-bargaining unit personnel who are themselves employees of the employer. Can a foreperson who is excluded from the bargaining unit by the terms of the recognition clause do some of the same work as an employee in the bargaining unit? If so, can that foreperson perform such work sporadically when an emergency arises or instruct and train others as a regular part of his or her job as foreperson? Some collective agreements provide express language to cover such a situation. Two representative clauses are as follows, each of which covers these two extremes:

Example 1

Non-bargaining unit employees will not regularly perform work which is normally performed by members of the bargaining unit except under the following conditions:

(a) **In emergencies where employees who are familiar with the work are not available;**

(b) **In the performance of necessary work when production difficulties are encountered on the job;**

(c) **For the purpose of instructing, training or relieving employees;**

(d) **For purposes of investigation of operating problems, maintenance needs, or new or changed methods.**

The union shall be notified when a non-bargaining unit employee performs more than four (4) hours bargaining unit work in a twenty-four (24) hour period.

Example 2

Forepersons and supervisors will not perform any work which is usually performed by those under their supervision, except in cases of emergency, emergency being breakdown or repair of machinery when no one is available to make the necessary repairs or in the absence of an employee or for the purpose of instructing employees.

It should be noted that in the first example the first sentence applies to "employees", which includes forepersons but also includes other categories of employees such as office or clerical persons. The restriction in the second sentence applies only to forepersons.

6. Union Representation

Most, if not all, collective agreements identify the particular union persons who have the responsibility to administer the application of the collective agreement on behalf of the union. The usual term for such a person is "steward" or "committee-person". Some collective agreements go further and set out the circumstances in which stewards and committee-persons may leave their normal work stations to attend to union business, the conditions under which they would continue to be paid their regular wages by the employer, as well as any limitations that may be imposed on this right or privilege. The collective agreement may also set out undertakings by the employer and by the union to require their respective representatives to co-operate with their opposite numbers in carrying out the terms and requirements of the collective agreement. An example of such an article is set out below:

.01 The company agrees to recognize one (1) steward per shift/location. The number of union stewards may be adjusted by mutual agreement. The steward's function shall be to process grievances which might arise in the zone or group he or she represents, according to the grievance procedure as hereinafter agreed to.

.02 It is agreed that a steward shall, after consultation with his or her foreperson, be permitted during working hours and without loss of pay, to leave his or her regular duties for a reasonable length of time in order to investigate and settle, if possible, any grievance which might arise in his or her group.

.03 The company shall recognize a union bargaining committee of four (4) full-time employees, represented from the following areas:

(1) Technical Services, i.e., Set Up/Press Service/Equipment Maintenance/Tool Room

(2) Warehouse

(3) Other

(4) Plant Chair

At the discretion of the union, international representatives shall also be recognized as members of the bargaining committee.

Employees so designated shall be paid their regular hourly rate for time spent at the negotiating meetings with the company, during their regularly scheduled working hours.

.04 The company and the union representatives shall meet when necessary to discuss and mutually settle any questions which might arise of importance to either party. Members who are on duty shall be paid their straight time rate of wages for that part of their regularly scheduled hours devoted to attendance at such meetings.

.05 No union-company business shall be discussed at a meeting of union-company representatives unless two (2) union bargaining committee members are present.

.06 The union shall notify the company of the names and office of all union members who have authority to represent the union, and mem-

bership with respect to negotiations, grievances and other matters arising out of this agreement, and their employment with the company.

With respect to the appointment or selection of the stewards or committee-persons, it is important to designate the number of persons who comprise the committee as well as the particular areas or departments from which they are chosen and for which they are responsible. In a large operation, it is not uncommon to have a steward or union representative from each of the different departments or plant areas. If more than one shift is involved, it may be appropriate to have stewards or representatives from each shift in each area. To some degree the manner of selection of union stewards or committee persons is determined by the union's by-laws or constitution, but it is in the interest of both parties to have adequate representation available to affected employees and to the employer to make the administration of the collective agreement work effectively.

Some collective agreements do specify the circumstances where the stewards may leave their work to attend to union business or where they must obtain someone's permission to do so. In some instances this may be unnecessary because the union representative in the plant has been placed on a leave of absence from the employer, and an office and other facilities have been provided so that the representative can have a separate location from the management on the premises from which to do union business. In the absence of that kind of arrangement, it is preferable to set out in the agreement a code of directions for union stewards who want to leave their work stations to attend to union business. This will help to avoid conflict between the exercise of the steward's responsibility to the union and his or her obligation as an employee to the employer. While there are many variations on the individual conditions by which a steward may leave work to attend to union business without loss of basic pay, the most common requisite is that the steward must first obtain permission from his or her immediate supervisor. Another contractual possibility to consider is that the employer has the right to limit the time away from work if it is excessive or if there is an abuse of the privilege.

7. Grievance Procedure and Arbitration

In a previous chapter this subject was discussed in the context of the statutory obligation of the parties to the collective agreement to set out a grievance and arbitration procedure to deal with differences as to the interpretation or application of the collective agreement that arise during the life of the agreement. The actual wording chosen must reflect a number of matters.

The premise for the parties is that there are going to be disputes during the life of the collective agreement that concern the interpretation or application of the agreement and they should have a mechanism that works effectively to resolve those disputes. Because of the wide variation in the size, complexity and sophistication of employers and unions, there is no simple formula that can be applied in all cases. However, there are a number of issues to be considered by the parties when drafting their particular grievance and arbitration article.

Dealing first with the grievance procedure, the parties may wish to highlight their intentions by expressing their agreement as to the importance of adjusting complaints and grievances as quickly as possible. But what is a grievance under that collective agreement? To answer that question, the parties may provide a definition of what may be the proper subject of a grievance. For example, a grievance may be defined as a matter which concerns the interpretation or alleged violation of the collective agreement. An alternative and broader definition is "a difference between the parties relating to the interpretation, application or administration of the collective agreement or an allegation that the collective agreement has been violated".

The next issue deals with any time limits as to when a grievance may be filed after something has occurred. Most collective agreements require that the grievance be filed within a specified number of days from the occasion which gave rise to the grievance. In some cases, this may be as short as two working days; in others it may be as long as a number of weeks. Some collective agreements also provide for a different time period where the matter concerns the pay of an employee. For example, if the grievance involves a discipline matter, the time period would normally run from the date of the imposition of the disciplinary penalty. On the other hand, if the grievance concerns a question of whether the employee was properly paid for a given day, the time period may not start to run until the employee has in fact received the pay cheque which covers the day or days in question. Finally, there may be a different time period to which the parties agree for the presentation of a grievance respecting the discharge of an employee.

Once the parties have decided on the time period for the presentation of grievances, a number of other matters must be addressed and appropriate language selected. Should the grievance be presented at the initial stage in oral form or must it be in writing? Should the grievance be presented by the grievor to the immediate supervisor and should the grievor have the right to have a steward present? How long should the supervisor who first receives the grievance have to consider an answer? Must the employer's response, as given by the supervisor, be in writing? How many further steps in the grievance procedure do the parties wish to establish? Who is to be present at the various grievance meetings, when are answers to the grievance to be given and in what form?

What is clearly the most important task for the parties in dealing with these specific questions is to structure a procedure that will work for them in the light of their own needs and their particular collective bargaining relationship. The purpose of the grievance procedure is to settle and resolve grievances, and the mechanism should be shaped in such a way that it works as effectively and as efficiently as possible. Thus, if the persons and representatives who have the real power to make decisions in resolving grievances are not present or involved at any stage of the grievance procedure, that in itself may mean that the procedure is not going to work satisfactorily. Similarly, if there are too many steps in the grievance procedure, this may impede the effective resolution of the grievance. To repeat, the objective is to establish a means to evaluate and hopefully resolve grievances, and the acid test of the grievance procedure is whether it is accomplishing this result.

If the grievance is not settled at an earlier stage of the grievance procedure, its resolution, unless abandoned by the party filing the grievance, must come through binding settlement by arbitration. Most collective agreements provide for the method of establishment of an arbitration tribunal, as well as some direction as to the tribunal's authority and jurisdiction in the event of certain kinds of grievance subjects such as discharge.

Generally, the parties have to decide whether their arbitration tribunal will be a board of arbitration or a sole arbitrator for determining all or certain defined kinds of grievances. If they select a board, they must set out the ground rules for the appointment of the board and the manner in which the two nominees select a third person to act as chair. If they decide on a sole arbitrator, they must provide how this person is to be selected and by whom. A number of collective agreements go further and set out a roster or panel of arbitrators who are named in the collective agreement to arbitrate grievances in rotation.

As to any direction about the arbitrator's jurisdiction, most collective agreements specify that the arbitrator will not have the power to change any of the terms of the collective agreement or to add to or modify any provision of the agreement. On the other side of the coin of authority, many collective agreements provide that in the event of a discharge or discipline case, the arbitrator has a wide discretion to vary the particular disciplinary penalty. A typical clause would set out the arbitrator's authority as follows:

(a) **confirming the management's action in dismissing the employee; or**
(b) **reinstating the employee with full compensation for time lost; or**
(c) **any other arrangement which is just and equitable in the opinion of the conferring parties or the board of arbitration.**

With respect to discharge and discipline cases, some collective agreements have a separate grievance article to provide a more expedited form of disposition of those grievances by initiating the process at the second or third stage of the grievance procedure. Further, the time periods for the grievance answers as well as the time period for putting the unresolved grievance to the arbitration stage may be shortened. The reason for such special treatment of discharge cases is the obvious urgency, from the employee's point of view, to have the grievance determined and get back to work. From the employer's side, there is potentially a continuing liability in back wages that requires a prompt decision.

Two other kinds of grievance articles appear in some collective agreements. One defines what may be the subject of a grievance presented by the employer. It will be recalled that the applicable labour relations statute requires that all differences between the parties shall be subject to resolution through binding arbitration. A collective agreement sets out a number of mutual obligations and rights between the employer, the union and the employees. It follows that the employer may decide to file a grievance alleging a violation of the collective agreement by the union or some of the employees. Some collective agreements set out such a right in contractual terms. An example of such a provision is as follows:

Any grievance instituted by management may be referred in writing to the plant committee within two (2) full working days of the occurrence of the circumstances giving rise to the grievance, and the plant committee shall meet within two (2) working days thereafter with management to consider the grievance. If final settlement of the grievance is not completed within five (5) working days of such meeting, the grievance may be referred, by either party, to a board of arbitration as provided in Article V at any time within ten (10) calendar days thereafter, but not later.

Another type of grievance would be the converse of the management grievance, namely, a grievance which affects the interest of the union as such and in regard to which an individual employee could not grieve. Such a grievance may be described as a policy grievance. An illustration of the proper subject of a policy grievance would be a dispute between the employer and the union arising from the alleged non-deduction of union dues. Some grievances may affect a large number of employees in the bargaining unit, and the way one grievance is decided would necessarily resolve the others. As a result, the parties may define what is the proper subject for a union policy grievance so as to avoid a multiplication of a large number of individual grievances which are identical in nature. Because policy grievances are often matters of high profile and general concern in the workplace, it may be appropriate to set out an expeditious procedure to deal with such a grievance, and to begin at a higher level in the grievance procedure. An example of a union policy grievance clause reads in this manner:

A union policy grievance, which is defined as an alleged violation of this agreement, concerning all or a substantial number of the employees in the bargaining unit, in regard to which an individual employee could not grieve, may be lodged by the chair of the grievance committee in writing with the plant manager at Step No. 2 of the grievance procedure at any time within two (2) full working days after the circumstances giving rise to such grievance occurred or originated; and if it is not satisfactorily settled, it may be processed to Step No. 3 and to arbitration in the same manner and to the same extent as the grievance of an employee.

Chapter 10

Other Language Issues

1. No Strikes — No Lock-outs

Legislation in all jurisdictions in Canada requires the parties to include a provision in a collective agreement that prohibits strikes and lock-outs while the agreement continues to operate. In certain collective agreements, the language the parties negotiate is simply a contractual undertaking that there will be no strikes or lock-outs during the term of the agreement.

While this may be sufficient to comply with the legislation, many collective agreements go further and define what constitutes a strike or lock-out, either by referring to the statute and incorporating that definition, or by expanding that definition in the language the parties negotiate. For instance, the parties may use words that go beyond the concept of "strike" and, for example, prohibit "picketing, slow-downs or stoppages of work, either complete or partial".

In other collective agreements, the parties may specify the sanctions to be applied in the event a violation of the no strike - no lock-out article takes place. For instance, there may be a provision that gives the employer the right to discipline employees who take part in or cause an unlawful or "wildcat" strike. This provision may be inserted in the collective agreement because the employer wishes to emphasize the serious nature of the consequences of such activities, or for informational purposes so that employees who are contemplating such action would know what might happen to them if they went on strike, or both. Such a provision might read as follows:

The company shall have the right to discharge or otherwise discipline employees who take part in or instigate any strike, picketing, stoppage or slow-down, but a claim of unjust discharge or discipline may be the subject of a grievance and dealt with as provided in Article VI above.

The union, on its part, may wish to provide a grievance mechanism to process a grievance where the union feels an unlawful lock-out has taken place. A lock-out invariably is a matter of high emotion and consequence, and the union may want to ensure that the grievance will be heard promptly. As a result, it might insist on a provision such as this:

Should the union claim that a cessation of work constitutes a lock-out, it may take the matter up with the company at Step No. 3 of the grievance procedure.

Another matter that may be the subject of negotiations when the negotiators are considering strikes and lock-outs is involving a party to the collective agreement in a dispute between the other party and an outside or third party. Thus, the employer may want assurance that the union will not involve the employer in a labour dispute between the union and some other employer. The usual term given to this kind of activity is a secondary boycott. If this is the case, the employer may seek a provision along the following lines:

The union agrees that it will not involve any employee of the company, or the company, either directly or indirectly in any dispute which may arise between any other employer and the employees of such other employer.

The union, of course, may have its own concerns, and seek protective language so that its members will not be required to work on products or material sent to the employer from another employer against whom that union or some other union is engaged in strike action. This is generally known as a "hot cargo" clause. In other situations, the parties may negotiate a clause directed at the right of the employer to require employees to cross a picket line established at another plant where a labour dispute is taking place. This problem can arise where employees of the first employer are sent to other work locations, or where, for example, truck drivers are required to deliver goods to customers. If the employees of a customer's plant are on a lawful strike and are picketing at the plant location, the employer may want its own employees to cross the picket line to deliver materials or supply services to the customer. But what if there is serious violence on the picket line? In some collective agreements, the employee is given an option to refuse to cross a picket line where there is a reasonable possibility of injury to the employee or to property. An example of the first type of clause is as follows:

It shall not be considered a violation of this agreement, however, if any member of the union should refuse to deliver materials to any project or location when an actual work stoppage or strike exists and a picket line or placard line has been established for the purpose of communicating the fact of such work stoppage or strike, providing such work stoppage or strike is not contrary to the provisions of the Ontario *Labour Relations Act.*

It is agreed that whenever any such situation occurs and a ready-

mix concrete pour has started, delivery may continue until such pour is completed, but in any event, not beyond a twenty-four (24) hour period after the actual work stoppage commences.

Union members shall not refuse to make deliveries through any picket line or placard line which is established for any other purpose or reason.

An example of a provision dealing with the crossing of picket lines where violent activity is taking place is as follows:

It shall not be considered a violation of this agreement for an employee to refuse to cross a lawful picket line where such employee has reasonable concern for his or her safety or where there is reasonable grounds for belief that damage to the employer's property or equipment may result from a crossing of such picket line.

2. Union Security

Depending on the attitudes of the parties toward each other and the nature of the relationship between them, the subject of union security may generate a good deal of collective bargaining heat. This, in part, is because union security deals with people's freedom to select a union of their own choice or an equally important right, the freedom to refuse to belong to a particular union or, indeed, any union.

In their first collective agreement following certification, the parties are likely to approach each other at the bargaining table at least with caution, if not mistrust. The union will normally want to secure its membership position with the employer and the employees that it represents, and insist on all employees either being required to join the union or at least paying dues to the union. The employer, on the other hand, is seldom interested in strengthening the union, especially since it is a new relationship, with doubts and uncertainties on all sides. The employer may want to establish a tactical advantage by keeping the union fragmented and as weak as possible. Finally, the employer may genuinely want to protect the freedom of choice of its employees, especially long-term employees who joined the organization long before any of them knew a union might be demanding they had to join in order to keep their jobs.

It is not the purpose of this book to engage in a philosophical discourse on the advantages of one form of union security in contrast to another. The point is that there probably are few other collective bargaining issues that are more open to debate and difficult to resolve for both employers and unions than union security, especially in a first collective agreement.

Union security appears in many forms, and there are a number of different concepts available for the parties to examine. The two main themes —

sometimes discussed separately, but logically linked — are union dues and union membership.

In ascending order, the weakest form of union security is a provision for a voluntary dues check-off. The principle behind this idea is that employees in the bargaining unit authorize the employer to deduct from their pay an amount equal to the union dues provided in the union constitution or by-laws. The employer, in turn, would be obliged to make the appropriate deduction each pay day from the wages paid to the employees, and the total sum from all the employees would be sent to the union on a periodic basis. The key is that an authorization from an employee to the employer to deduct the dues is personal and voluntary.

Even if the parties agree to a voluntary check-off arrangement, certain additional questions must be answered. While the original authorization may be voluntary, can it later be revoked by the employee and, if so, when? If the authorization can be revoked at any point by the employee, such an arrangement is called a voluntary revocable check-off. Under a different kind of arrangement, the employee may sign a dues authorization card at any time during the life of the collective agreement, but the authorization, once signed, cannot be revoked. A further variation is to establish what is called an "escape period", which is a specified period of time, usually at the end of the collective agreement, during which employees may revoke or cancel their authorizations. Revocations that are submitted at any other time would be invalid.

An example of a voluntary revocable check-off for the deduction of union dues is as follows:

> **The company agrees, during the lifetime of this agreement, to the extent authorized in writing by each employee, but not otherwise, to deduct whatever sum may be authorized for union dues from the first pay due each calendar month, and to remit same not later than the last day of the same month to the financial secretary of the local union. Any such authorization shall be in duplicate and shall be signed by the employee concerned and properly witnessed. It shall be on a form prepared by the union and approved by the company and shall take effect after fifteen (15) days from the date of signing. Such authorization may be revoked in writing by the employee concerned at any time but such revocation shall not take effect until fifteen (15) days after the same has been filed with the company. One (1) copy of any such authority or revocation shall be filed with the paymaster and one (1) copy given to the financial secretary of the local union. The company shall, when remitting such dues, name the employees from whose pay such deductions have been made, and also the names of any employees who have revoked such authority since the last payment, or who have left the employ of the company.**

The next form of union security requires the deduction of union dues, but specifies that the deduction be compulsory for all employees in the bargaining unit. Thus, the deduction is no longer voluntary, and the union dues are automatically deducted from an employee's wages simply because he or she is employed in the bargaining unit.

One variation on this theme is sometimes referred to as the Rand Formula. The concept is that employees are not required to become and remain members of the union as a condition of employment, but all employees in the bargaining unit will have deducted from their regular pay an amount equal to the union dues, and this money must then be forwarded by the employer to the union. The argument in justification of the Rand Formula is that the union is obliged by law to represent all employees in the bargaining unit. For instance, the union must process legitimate grievances of employees who are subject to the collective agreement, whether the particular grievor is a member of the union or not. Similarly, when the union negotiates increases in wages or benefits, these apply to all employees in the bargaining unit, without regard to their union membership. Therefore, the logic goes, all persons in the bargaining unit should make some financial contribution to the cost of maintaining and operating the union, even though they may elect not to become members.

An illustration of this form of union security appears below:

During the lifetime of this agreement the company shall deduct from the pay of all employees covered by this agreement on the first pay day of each calendar month the amount of the regular monthly dues payable by all members of the union as certified by the financial secretary of the union. The said sums shall be accepted by the union as the regular monthly dues of those employees who are or shall become members of the union, and the sum so deducted from non-members of the union shall be treated as their contribution towards the expenses of maintaining the union.

In Ontario, at least some of the negotiating pressure was released by an amendment to the *Labour Relations Act* in 1980. Section 43 of the Act effectively incorporates in legislative form the Rand Formula. The section reads as follows:

43.(1) Except in the construction industry and subject to section 47, where a trade union that is the bargaining agent for employees in a bargaining unit so requests, there shall be included in the collective agreement between the trade union and the employer of the employees a provision requiring the employer to deduct from the wages of each employee in the unit affected by the collective agreement, whether or not the employee is a member of the union, the amount of the regular union dues and to remit the amount to the trade union, forthwith.

(2) In subsection (1), "regular union dues" means,

(a) in the case of an employee who is a member of the trade union, the dues uniformly and regularly paid by a member of the trade union in accordance with the constitution and by-laws of the trade union; and

(b) in the case of an employee who is not a member of the trade union, the dues referred to in clause (a), excluding any amount in respect of pension, superannuation, sickness insurance or any other benefit available only to members of the trade union.

As a result, the invariable practice in bargaining any collective agreement in Ontario, including a first agreement, is that the union makes a formal request under the section and the employer must agree to a dues check-off arrangement in the resulting collective agreement.

The preceding forms of union security have dealt with the question of union dues or an equivalent deduction. There are, of course, other forms of union security which impose certain obligations with respect to union membership. These arrangements vary, depending upon the relationship and bargaining objectives of the parties and the practice in the particular industry.

The mildest form of union security that deals with the question of union membership is a requirement, called a maintenance of membership provision, that all employees who are members of the union at the time the collective agreement comes into force or who later become members of the union are required to remain members in good standing during the lifetime of the agreement as a condition of employment. The latter phrase, that is, "a condition of employment", means a requirement or obligation that must be met if a person wishes to keep his or her job with that employer. One variation of this maintenance of membership provision is a time period at the start of the collective agreement during which employees can resign from the union without losing their jobs. An example of this provision is as follows:

All employees who fifteen (15) days after the execution of this agreement are members of the union in good standing and all employees who thereafter become members, shall as a condition of employment remain members of the union in good standing during the lifetime of this agreement.

The union shall promptly furnish to the company a certified list of its members in good standing as of the fifteenth (15th) day after the execution of this agreement. If any employee named on the list asserts that he or she withdrew from membership within the union prior to that

day, and any dispute arises, or if any dispute arises as to whether an employee is or is not a member of the union in good standing, the question as to withdrawal or good standing, as the case may be, shall be adjudicated by a board of arbitration pursuant to the arbitration provisions of this agreement, and the decision of such board shall be final and binding on the union, the employee and the company.

The next form of union security to be considered is commonly described as a union shop. Under this arrangement, each employee in the bargaining unit must join the union and remain a member in good standing during the lifetime of the collective agreement as a condition of employment. While some collective agreements provide that this obligation is triggered as soon as the employee becomes employed, the majority of collective agreements that provide for a union shop have a time period, often the length of the probationary period, before the employee must join the union. An example of a union shop clause is as follows:

All present employees in the bargaining unit who have acquired seniority shall become and remain members in good standing of the union during the lifetime of this agreement as a condition of employment, and all persons who may hereafter become employees in the bargaining unit shall immediately upon expiration of their probationary period become and remain members in good standing of the union during the lifetime of this agreement as a condition of employment.

The final form of union security to be discussed is the closed shop. This arrangement is common in the construction industry and in some industries where craft unions predominate. A closed shop — that is, a system where the employer can hire only union members — makes sense if the union is able to supply the employer with trained and qualified personnel when the employer needs additional employees. To protect itself against the possibility that the union will not have qualified persons who can be dispatched immediately to the work location, the employer may demand a short, fixed time period within which the union must respond to the employer's demand for personnel. If the union is unable to fill the employer's request, the employer is free to hire people from any available source. However, the person who is hired by the employer from the street where the union was unable to supply a qualified person would still have to join the union within a specified number of days in order to keep working for that employer.

By way of illustration, a closed shop provision reads as follows:

All present employees and all future employees must upon the completion of their probationary period become and remain members in

good standing of the union during the lifetime of this agreement as a condition of employment.

In the hiring of new employees, the company agrees to hire only persons who are members of the union and these shall be hired from lists supplied by the union. The union undertakes to supply the company with competent help. If, within forty-eight (48) hours after a request has been made by the company to the union, the union shall fail to provide the required help, then the company will be at liberty to engage such help from the open market, but in such case the person so employed shall at the expiration of his or her probationary period become and remain a member of the union for the lifetime of the agreement as a condition of employment.

Even though it has agreed to any one of a maintenance of membership, closed shop or union shop provision, the employer may be legitimately concerned about the possibility of losing an employee who has been expelled from union membership on frivolous grounds, or as the result of internal union politics. Presumably, the employer would not want to have to fire a valued employee because of difficulties that arise between that employee and the union. Therefore, the employer may want to add to the standard union shop clause the following language:

Notwithstanding anything contained in this article, the company shall not be required to discharge any employee to whom membership in the union has been denied or terminated on some ground other than the refusal of such employee to tender the initiation fee and dues uniformly required in order to acquire or maintain membership in the union, unless the company agrees that the grounds upon which the union refused or terminated such employee's membership are valid, or in the alternative, unless the matter is referred to arbitration in the manner hereinafter prescribed by this agreement, and a board of arbitration decides that the grounds upon which the union refused or terminated the membership of such employee were sufficient to justify his or her discharge by the company.

3. Seniority

A number of arbitrators have stated that the concept of seniority is the foundation of the collective agreement and vital to the employees covered by the agreement. As a result, representatives of employers and unions necessarily spend much time and care negotiating seniority provisions in all their complicated glory.

To begin with, there is inevitably a tension between the needs of the employer, the union, and most importantly, the employees, when seniority applies to any job opportunity situation. This tension is generated by the fact that the employer will want to have the most effective and efficient workforce at any point in time. However, the most senior employees are not always the most efficient persons at work. From the employee's perspective, long service with the employer is a form of increasing equity in the job. If someone is to be displaced, this should happen only if the person claiming the job has more seniority than the employee who already has the job. The respective negotiators have to reach a form of compromise or balance between the legitimate, but competing interests of the employer and the employees in the battle of seniority rights.

When considering seniority, the parties must determine both the definition of seniority, that is, how one gets and accumulates seniority, and to what use seniority can be put, that is, how seniority will be applied. There are at least three different kinds of seniority that the parties can consider.

The first is plant-wide or bargaining unit seniority. Under this system, all employees in the bargaining unit accumulate seniority based on length of service in the bargaining unit. All are treated as a single group for the purpose of acquiring seniority, and each person's seniority in the bargaining unit is ranked with everyone else.

The second may be called departmental seniority. The employer's operation is divided into different groupings for the purpose of acquiring individual seniority rights. Thus, an employee's departmental seniority date is the date the employee first worked in that department. The parties must define the boundaries of these particular groups but, conceptually, they can establish as many separate compartments as they wish. Employees are ranked for seniority purposes within their own defined group. An employee can have more than one seniority date, for example, both plant-wide and departmental seniority. Plant or bargaining unit seniority can be applied for some purposes and, in other circumstances, departmental seniority may be used.

A third kind of seniority arrangement is seniority by job classification. In a sense this is an extension of the departmental seniority approach, with the job classification being the equivalent of a particular department. Thus, each employee is ranked for the purpose of accumulating seniority with other employees in his or her own job classification based upon the date the employee first worked in that classification.

The next problem for the parties, once they have decided on the form and definition of seniority, is when an employee obtains seniority. In other words, how long should the probationary period be? When a new employee is hired, the employer will want time to evaluate that person's performance to decide whether to put the employee in the permanent workforce. Traditionally, most unions have recognized that the employer should be given a period of time to make an appraisal. The employee would not have seniority rights, and consequently the right to full job protection, until the end of the probationary period and the new employee is confirmed as a permanent employee. The length of the probationary period may vary from a few days to a number of weeks or months. Whatever period of time is agreed upon, the collective agreement should specify what contractual rights, if any, the probationary employee has under the collective agreement while he or she is employed as a probationer. If the parties do not specify the rights of a probationary employee, any right of an employee is also the right of a probationer. For example, should a probationer receive the full job rate in a given classification, or is there a special learner's rate? What fringe benefits does he or she receive? Is the decision to discharge a probationer to be within the exclusive discretion of the employer, or will a probationer have access to arbitration to dispute the decision not to put the employee in the permanent workforce? A typical clause reads as follows:

An employee will be considered on probation for the first two (2) months and will have no seniority rights during that period. After two (2) months' service, his or her seniority shall date back to the day on which his or her employment began. The dismissal, lay-off or failure to recall after lay-off of a probationary employee is within the sole discretion of the employer and shall not be the subject of a grievance.

The next significant area of concern is the weight to be given seniority and the circumstances in which seniority is a factor in decisions affecting specific employment rights. The most common application of seniority is with respect to lay-offs and recalls from lay-off. In addition, seniority may be a significant factor in promotions and transfers.

In describing what is to happen in the event of lay-offs and recalls from lay-off, the parties may exclude certain types of lay-offs, usually of short-term duration. For instance, some collective agreements provide that "lay-offs that are anticipated not to exceed five (5) working days" do not require seniority to be applied in determining the individuals to be laid off. Apart from the definition of lay-offs that will result in the application of seniority, the parties must then specify what weight to give seniority in relation to other factors in the decision making process as to who is to be laid off or recalled from lay-off. The point is the application of seniority does not affect the justification or correctness of a decision to have a lay-off; however, it is a factor, sometimes the crucial one, in the selection of the particular persons who go out the door once the decision is made that there are too many employees to do the available work.

4. Factors in Addition to Seniority

Under some collective agreements, seniority is the only factor or criterion to be considered in deciding who goes and who stays. This is the case particularly where seniority is a factor applied on a job classification basis. Presumably all of the employees in each classification are qualified, or they would not be working in such classification. According to this reasoning, if a lay-off of some of the persons in that classification is required, seniority is the only factor to be considered. Whether the seniority date to be applied is an employee's plant-wide seniority date or departmental seniority date is a matter to be agreed upon by the parties.

Many collective agreements provide that seniority must be considered, and also set out additional criteria to be given weight along with seniority. The collective agreement may provide that such factors as skill, efficiency, ability or competence are to be weighed between the employees who are being considered for the lay-off. If the employees are relatively equal, seniority determines who is to be laid off and who is to be retained. If this approach is to be used, language such as the following would be appropriate:

Lay-offs shall be based upon the following factors:

(a) seniority;

(b) skill, competence, efficiency and ability.

Where the qualifications in factor (b) are relatively equal, seniority shall govern.

Another approach is that the parties negotiate a provision which is not a contest or evaluation between individuals but matches the qualifications of the employees considered for lay-off against the requirements of the work to be performed once the lay-off occurs. If two or more employees have the necessary qualifications, the decision as to who is to be laid off would be based on seniority. An example of this kind of clause is as follows:

Should it become necessary to lay off employees from the plant due to lack of work, the employees with the least plant seniority will be the first laid off provided the employees retained are capable of doing the work and provided also that such lay-offs do not necessitate promotion in order to balance the crew. The company agrees to notify the union whenever a job is being discontinued.

The last employee laid off will be the first recalled provided the employee is qualified to do the work and he or she has retained seniority.

Depending of course on the language of the particular collective agreement, the fact that someone is initially selected for lay-off from a specific job may not in fact result in the actual lay-off of that person. It may be that the individual displaced from one job has the right to select someone else's job and to "bump" the employee who has that job, who in turn may displace another employee in another job, until finally someone is laid off. Such an arrangement is not uncommon where seniority is on a departmental basis and there are other jobs in other departments that are not being considered for lay-off. While there are many variations, one example is set out below:

Lay-offs and Recalls

.01 With the exception of employees in Preferred Classifications as outlined in Appendix B and employees in Skilled Trades Classifications as outlined in Appendix D, reductions in the workforce will be carried out in accordance with the following procedures provided in each case that the employee affected is willing and has the ability to perform the work available.

(a) **A lay-off of any employee or employees by the company for a period of three (3) days or less at any time at the discretion of the company may be made within a department except that no one (1) employee shall be laid off more than four (4) times or more than twelve (12) days in any one (1) calendar year. For the purpose of conducting a lay-off within a department the following shall apply:**

  1. **Probationary employees within the department shall be laid off first.**
  2. **Thereafter departmental seniority within the department shall apply.**
  3. **Lay-off for the purpose of taking inventory shall not be included in the above calculations, but shall not exceed one (1) day per inventory and a maximum of three (3) times per year.**

(b) **In the event of a lay-off for a period of more than three (3) working days, the following procedure will govern.**

  1. **In any department where the workforce is reduced probationary employees will be laid off first.**
  2. **As further reductions in the workforce are made in a department, regular employees will be assigned in reverse order of seniority to displace probationary employees in other departments.**
  3. **As further reductions in the workforce are made in a department, employees who have the requisite seniority shall be assigned to fill openings created by the lay-off of the required number of least senior employees throughout the plant.**
  4. **In the application of this section interchange between light and heavy operations will not be permitted except that employees who**

do not have the requisite seniority to exercise their seniority rights throughout the plant in accordance with the above procedure may be assigned to fill openings created by the lay-off of the required number of least senior employees employed in light and heavy operations throughout the plant.

.02 An employee who is displaced from his or her present classification as a result of a reduction in the workforce may, in lieu of exercising his or her seniority rights, accept a lay-off and retain seniority rights within the terms of this agreement.

Once an employee accepts a lay-off in lieu of exercising seniority as provided above, he or she does not have the right to return to work to displace another employee until he or she is recalled by the company when work is available in the classification from which he or she was laid off.

.03 In the event of a reduction of work within a Preferred Classification as outlined in Appendix B, employees will be laid off in reverse order of their seniority. In the event that an employee in a Preferred Classification is displaced from such Preferred Classification by an employee with greater seniority in the same Preferred Classification in his or her department or section he or she will then exercise his or her seniority in accordance with Section .01(b)(2) and .01(b)(3).

While the clause that deals with the circumstances in which seniority is to be applied is the real essence of the seniority article, there are other subjects that must be dealt with in order to make the seniority article work. For instance, the parties will want to describe how seniority is accumulated and in what circumstances it is terminated. As to the former, the usual approach is seniority accumulates, at the very least, while the employee is working, and continues to accumulate during absences due to lay-off, sickness or accident, personal leave of absence or vacation, although there may be a time limit after which further accumulation will cease. Thus, the collective agreement may state that seniority will accumulate during the first six months of a lay-off but not thereafter. This does not mean that the employee loses seniority that has been previously acquired. What it does mean is that, on returning to work, the employee is credited with six months' additional seniority, even though the lay-off may have lasted several months in excess of that period.

Seniority terminates, under most collective agreements, when the employee voluntarily quits his or her employment, or is discharged and not reinstated through the grievance procedure or arbitration. Many collective agreements go beyond this and provide that if the lay-off or absence from work as a result of illness is longer than, say, twenty-four months, seniority terminates at that point. Other collective agreements may state that seniority terminates if the employee fails to report for work within a specified number of days after being notified by the employer of recall from lay-off, or if the employee fails to return upon the termination of an authorized leave of absence, unless a satisfactory reason is given.

There are other aspects of seniority to be found in many collective agreements. For example, there may be a provision requiring employees to notify the employer of a change of address so that notices of recall can be correctly sent to them by mail. There may be a clause dealing with the seniority rights of an employee who for some period of time has been promoted to a position beyond the scope of the collective agreement, such as foreperson, and then returns to the unit. The purpose of this clause would be to outline what additional seniority credits, if any, are to be added to the seniority the employee previously acquired while in the bargaining unit, to cover the period of time spent outside the unit. As well, there may be a provision concerning an employee's reinstatement after sick leave, and under what conditions an employee may return to work. Finally, there should be a system for identifying and tracking the respective seniority dates of employees. The usual method is for the employer to compile seniority lists based upon the definition of seniority in the collective agreement and to post such lists on the bulletin board on a periodic basis.

5. Job Posting

Under some collective agreements, a job posting provision is placed in the seniority article. Because of the importance of the subject, it is more frequently found in a separate article of its own. Generally speaking, the job posting article sets out an arrangement whereby employees are advised of the existence of job vacancies and are given an opportunity to identify to the employer their interest in being selected to fill the vacancy.

The selection from the applicants for the job may be based on seniority only, or it may be based on seniority in combination with other factors. In many collective agreements, the same basic criteria are applied in a job posting situation as are used under the collective agreement in deciding who is to be laid off. Thus, if seniority is only one of the factors in determining who is to be laid off, it is likely that the collective agreement will provide the same approach in a job posting situation.

As a consequence, there are two basic types of job posting clauses. The first is a provision that requires the employer to evaluate the applicants in relation to each other, on the basis of criteria, such as skills or qualifications, specified in the collective agreement. If two or more of the applicants are relatively equal, the seniority factor determines who fills the vacancy. An example of this kind of provision is as follows:

.01 Should a vacancy occur in any classification other than an entry level classification, the employer agrees to post on the appropriate bulletin board a notice of such vacancy for four (4) days. An employee desiring a position in these classifications will be allowed to bid on them. The selection of an employee to fill the vacancy will be made from the employees who bid for the job who have completed their probationary periods whenever possible. The vacancy will be filled based upon the applicant's skill, ability and physical capability to do the job. Where the qualifications are relatively equal, the applicant with the most seniority will be given the job. If no qualified employee is available, the employer may hire a person to fill the vacancy.

The second kind of job posting provision simply requires the applicant to have the necessary qualifications to fill the job in question. If there are two or more persons who have the necessary qualifications, the most senior applicant is given the job. An example of this kind of clause is as follows:

.01 All permanent vacancies shall be posted on a bulletin board for a period of three (3) working days. Employees may apply for posted vacancies by written application within said three (3) working days. Only the original vacancy shall be posted. Subsequent vacancies need not be posted and may be filled by the most senior qualified person. A successful applicant for a posted vacancy shall not be eligible to apply for another posted vacancy for a period of six (6) months except in cases where the vacancy being bid is in a higher job class than the employee's present job or the job opening is an apprenticeship. A copy of all job bids will be given to the Union President if requested.

.02 The company and the union agree that those applicants with the greatest seniority shall be given preference for posted jobs providing that the employees involved possess the skill, ability and efficiency to do the work required.

Some collective agreements require the employer to post notice of the vacancy, in order to inform the employees that the vacancy exists and to give them a chance to show their interest in the job by signing the posting. However, the language may go on to provide that the employer is not obliged to select from among the applicants if no qualified persons apply. An example of this kind of clause is set out below:

All permanent vacancies in new classifications and in existing classifications shall be posted in the plant for a period of five (5) days and any employee in the bargaining unit in a lower rated classification may make application for such vacancy. In the filling of the vacancies, the company shall not be limited to selecting employees who have made application. Nothing herein shall prevent the company from hiring persons from outside the bargaining unit when no qualified employee applies. Any vacancy can be filled at the discretion of the company on a temporary basis. In the event that an employee has been selected to fill such a permanent vacancy then at any time within five (5) working days after being assigned to such vacancy he or she may elect to revert to his or her old classification, and if he or she does so then he or she shall be precluded from applying for any new vacancy for a period of six (6) calendar months. Only the original vacancy shall be posted and all vacancies which may occur as a result of having filled the original vacancy shall be filled at the discretion of the company.

Chapter 11

Some Cost Issues Including Wages

Each time the employer complies with most of the obligations in the various provisions of a collective agreement there is a direct economic cost to that employer. In some instances, such as wages, the cost can be easily calculated and measured as a projection of how many dollars will be paid out during the lifetime of the collective agreement. In other cases, such as vacations, there are both direct costs and indirect costs which are more difficult to evaluate.

To illustrate, the cost of a particular vacation program that grants the same number of vacation days, dependent on length of service, varies from one employer to another, since the seniority mix of the employees and the specific number of employees will be different. Similarly, a collective agreement that provides an additional week's vacation to employees who have attained twenty-five years of service is of minimal cost importance if there are only one or two employees in that category. On the other hand, employees must be found to replace other persons who are on vacation. Since the employer cannot know in advance when they will be on vacation, the indirect cost of an increase in vacation benefits can only be guessed at. There is no way to establish precisely the cost of implementing a bereavement leave clause over the term of the collective agreement for the obvious reason that one cannot forecast how many employees will suffer a death in their families in the future months or years during which the agreement will operate.

1. Costing of Monetary Matters

Before dealing with a number of individual cost items, some general observations should be made. To begin with, both employers and unions have come to recognize that the direct and indirect cost of monetary items must be considered, at least to a degree, as a total cost package. At one time some employer negotiators were prepared to deal with individual cost items in isolation without recognizing that each cost item, once agreed to, was effectively an accumulating dollar total. Thus, the parties might negotiate a number of welfare program improvements without regard to other outstanding cost items such as wages. When the time came to deal with wages, the employer would be startled to find that it had already agreed to improvements to the welfare package with a direct cost to it of most, if not all, of the available funds for the entire collective agreement. More recently, both employer and union negotiators have recognized that agreement on part of the cost package has a direct and obvious bearing on the other parts and that cost items must be viewed as a total package.

In addition, there sometimes is confusion as to how to calculate the cost of a given collective agreement provision. The simplest way to make this calculation is to add up the total dollar costs, over the life of the collective agreement, of each of the improvements that have been negotiated, based on the number of employees, their length of service and the employer's prior experience in similar situations, and then reduce that total sum to a cents per hour per employee basis. As noted, some of these figures can be accurately projected, but for others an estimate must be made as to how many times an event, say, a bereavement, is likely to happen.

If the collective agreement is for a one-year period and wages are the only cost item that has been negotiated, it is a simple matter to establish the cost of the settlement. If vacations have been improved, in addition to wage increases, the employer would have to determine by reference to the individual seniority groupings of its employees how many persons would be affected by the improved vacation benefits and to what extent. If the total sum per year for such vacation improvements was, say, $10,000, that figure would have to be translated into a cents per hour per employee calculation by dividing the $10,000 by the number of employees and converting it to an hourly figure. This is usually accomplished by expressing the total number of hours that each employee would be expected to work in a year as 2040 hours per year per employee. Thus the formula would be:

$$\frac{\$10,000 \div 2040 \text{ (hours)}}{\times \text{ (number of employees)}}$$

If the collective agreement is for a longer period of time, that fact must be built into the cost projections. In addition, there may be an "impact" cost involved. An impact cost can arise in at least two ways. In the first place, if there are two or more wage increases during the period of the collective agreement, the wage cost will be impacted in the second increase. For instance, if the first wage increase is 8%, such increase will be calculated at 8% times the existing wage rate paid to employees immediately before the negotiated increase went into effect. If the second wage increase is also 8%, that increase, depending on the wording of the collective agreement, will be applied to the then current wages which have already been increased by the first 8%. Thus, the second increase, expressed in straight percentage terms, would be

8%, but the cost to the employer would be the original base figure of 100 increased by the first 8%, or 8% of 108.

A second way in which costs are impacted results from the interrelationship of the various components of the contractual obligations. In the example previously given of a one-year collective agreement with an 8% wage increase, the costing must reflect the fact that overtime will be worked during the new collective agreement year. Thus, the employer would be obliged to pay an overtime premium, or a multiple of each specific wage rate which had been increased by 8%. While it is difficult to be precise in determining how much overtime will be worked in the next year, the prudent employer would estimate the amount of overtime that can be reasonably anticipated in order to make a cost evaluation of what an 8% wage increase amounts to in terms of overtime rates. Similarly, as the wages increase, so does the cost of the fringe benefits payable under the terms of the collective agreement. Statutory holiday pay usually is based on the existing hourly rate of the employee, which in turn, in the illustration given, has been increased by 8%. Again, vacation pay would be calculated either as a percentage of total wages earned during the vacation year or on the basis of an average week's pay. In either event, that figure would have been increased by the application of the wage increase that had been negotiated.

While it is not feasible to examine every conceivable cost issue, we will look at the more common monetary provisions found in collective agreements. First, a word of caution: the full assessment of any particular cost item depends on a number of variables, such as orders that may or may not materialize, success or failure in marketing new products and so on, but the principles that are reviewed are applicable to most collective bargaining relationships.

2. Wages

To many persons, the key provision in any collective agreement is the wage to be paid to any particular employee. While it may seem a straightforward task to negotiate what this rate should be, there are a number of collective bargaining considerations that must be addressed other than the wage figure itself.

The first observation to make is that it is fundamental to identify which employees will be receiving a given wage rate and, in most cases, to differentiate between them where more than one wage rate is paid. Some collective agreements state in the wage schedule or article that all employees in the bargaining unit will receive a wage increase of so many cents per hour or a specified percentage amount above the current wage rate paid to them at the commencement of the collective agreement. However, most collective agreements go further and set out in the wage schedule either the job titles or job groupings together with other information. For example, the schedule may set out the starting rate together with a job progression outline plotting the path by which a given employee proceeds from one rate to another within a classification or, in some cases, from one classification to another.

Two different terms are frequently used from time to time as interchangeable, resulting in much confusion. Job titles or classifications are descriptive labels which identify a given job being performed by an employee or group of employees. Job descriptions are a catalogue of the duties and a summary of the tasks to be performed by each employee or group of employees. The job title identifies the job, while the job description describes in brief form the work content of the job. Both concepts are notions that are separate from the wage rate to be paid for the job.

If the employer has a relatively small operation, it may be that the jobs in the operation can be listed under a few job titles or headings. If the employer has a somewhat larger complement, it may be impractical to list each and every job under a separate job title. Thus, the employer and the union may select a more general or generic job title to cover a number of individual jobs. There may be a number of punch presses of different sizes used in a particular operation but the parties may establish the title of "punch press operator" which includes all of the individual operators of all of the punch presses. An even more general approach, rather than ascribing to each operator a designation or title for each machine, is to use a catch-all title such as "small machine operator". Parties to a collective agreement should be careful in their use of such fuzzy designations. The broader and more vague is a particular title, the more it may give rise to misunderstandings concerning who is covered by it. Simply put, the parties should ensure that they clearly understand what specific jobs are covered by the title they have selected.

To extend the point, a number of job titles may be conveniently grouped under an overall group heading. One of the collective bargaining aims of most unions is to achieve standardization, or at least substantial equalization, of wage rates and to avoid a multiplicity of individual job rates. To accomplish this, many collective agreements identify a group or groups under each of which a number of individual jobs are listed by title. If this form of wage schedule is chosen, to determine what is the rate for a given job one looks first at the job title and then finds where that title appears under the particular group heading. While the particular job title arrangement may be set out by the negotiating parties on whatever basis they wish, it is imperative, in order to avoid disputes, that they devise a structure that is clear and graphic. At the very least, the job titles should cover all of the jobs being performed in the bargaining unit and there should be express agreement as to which job has what title.

Apart from whether there are job titles or groupings in the collective agreement, other factors come into play. Is a new employee to be hired at the same rate as an experienced person in that same job? Most collective agreements provide for a lower differential for new employees, either on a percentage or cents per hour basis. If that is the case, after what period of time does the employee progress to the full rate? Again, most collective agreements answer this question, at least in part, by stating that the employee will advance to the next stage in the rate structure upon completion of the probationary period. The next question to be considered is what happens after that point? Are all employees who have attained seniority and who are similarly classified to be paid the same job rate, or are more experienced employees to be paid more, depending on their length of service?

Many collective agreements provide for a job progression scheme whereby an employee in a particular job is advanced to a higher rate as the person's service and experience increases in that job. The intervals may be expressed in segments of weeks, months or years, but the negotiators must be precise in setting out that progression. In addition, the parties must concern themselves with the manner in which an employee proceeds from one step in the wage progression to another. For instance, does an employee advance from one wage level to another only upon the passage of a specified period of time, or does the employer have discretion in advancing that employee to another wage level? If it is the former, this is commonly known as an automatic wage progression, in the sense that the period of advancing service itself determines the wage level of an employee at any point in time. One need only look at the classification and length of service of any employee to determine what is the proper wage level and rate for that employee. Some collective agreements, however, not only provide that an employee must have a prescribed length of service in the job, but may set out a discretionary right on the part of the employer to decide when an employee will be advanced.

While most collective agreements set out a specific wage to be paid to an employee performing a given job, some provide a range of wage rates for that job. The collective agreement may state that employees who fall into a given job category are to be paid a rate between two specified wage figures. The difficulty with this arrangement is that arguments may arise as to the appropriate basis of wage differentiation in making decisions as to the wage rates of different employees performing the same job. For this reason, many employers and unions have tried to describe in the wage schedule a precise form of job and wage identification together with the progression rates, if any, and the trigger dates by which an employee proceeds through each of the steps of the job progression scheme.

In addition to what has been said, other matters may also be dealt with under the wage schedule. Some collective agreements provide for a premium rate to be paid to leadhands or non-managerial employees who perform limited supervisory functions. While the premium to be paid may be set out in a separate article, it is usually found under the wage schedule. The method by which the premium is expressed should be clear. For instance, if the wage rates are set out as an hourly rate, the premium should also be set out as so many cents per hour. Apart from this, the language should address whether the premium amount is to be added, for example, to the rate of the highest paid employee in the group being supervised by the leadhand. It is also helpful if the wording determines whether the premium is to be paid for each hour worked, or whether there is to be pyramiding for overtime purposes. To make this clear, assume that the leadhand premium is 40¢ per hour. The issue is whether the leadhand gets this sum for each hour worked, including each overtime hour, or whether that employee receives time and one-half the hourly wage rate to which has been added the 40¢ per hour premium. While this may seem at first glance a negligible difference, depending on the size of the employer's operation, the number of employees receiving such premium, and the extent of overtime hours worked, it may amount to a significant amount over the term of the collective agreement.

Some examples of wage schedules taken from different collective agreements illustrate the points that have been made:

Example 1

Schedule "A"

(A) Wage Rates

Effective 86 05 01

Miscellaneous Labour

Job Title	Job Rate
Launderer 1	$ 9.31
Labourer	10.00
Porter	10.02
Watchman/Woman	10.02
Porter/Expeditor	10.11
Launderer 2	10.25
Groundskeeper	10.25
Storekeeper	10.25
Shipper/Receiver	10.25
Driver	10.28
Delivery/Materials Handler	10.54
Senior Storekeeper	10.69
Grounds Machinery Operator	10.85
Gardener	11.07
Pest Control Assistant	11.07
Nurserykeeper and Greenhouse Technician	11.64

Heavy Equipment Operator	11.64
Sanitation Equipment Operator	11.82

Housekeeping

Building Custodian 1	$ 9.31
Building Custodian 2	9.77
Building Custodian 3	10.25
Building Custodian 4	10.70
Building Custodian 5	11.68
Lead Hand Building Custodian 1 to 4	11.17
Operations Development Assistant	11.17

Trades

Painter	$12.75
Spray Painter	13.14
Glazier	13.14
Plasterer	13.14
Mason/Bricklayer	13.14
Locksmith	13.14
Sheet Metal Worker	13.14
Blacksmith	13.14
Vehicle Mechanic	13.14
Carpenter	13.14
Carpet Installer/Upholsterer	13.14
Carpenter Millwright	13.64
Controls Mechanic	13.64
Machinist Millwright	13.64
Electrician	13.64
Plumber/Steamfitter	13.64
Instrument Mechanic	13.64
Senior Vehicle Mechanic	13.64
Sign Painter	13.64
Refrigeration Mechanic	13.64
Helper 1	10.00
Helper 2	10.76
Helper 3	90% of appropriate trade rate
Building Mechanic 1	11.30
Building Mechanic 2	12.24
Building Mechanic 3	13.14
Building Mechanic 4	13.64
Housekeeping Equipment Serviceperson	10.30
Housekeeping Equipment Mechanic	13.14

Grounds Mechanic 12.10

PROBATIONARY EMPLOYEES — $0.20/hour lower than the rate for which they were hired

LEADHAND EMPLOYEES — appropriate rate plus $0.20/hour

Fire Prevention Officers

Probation Rate	After 1 Year	After 2 Years	After 3 Years
$11.18	$11.76	$12.26	$12.83

1. The increase outlined above must be recommended by the Chief and the Safety and Security Department Head. Where an increase on the basis of time served is not recommended:

(a) the Director of Personnel or nominee in the Personnel Department must be satisfied as to the validity of the reasons for withholding such recommendation;

(b) the employee concerned must be informed as to the reasons why the increase is withheld, the improvements in performance which are expected and the time period after which the employee will be reconsidered for the increase.

Grievances arising out of this paragraph may be instituted at Step 3 of the Grievance Procedure.

2. New employees may be hired at a rate above the starting rate indicated on the basis of prior experience.

3. Any employee may be awarded one (1) or more additional increments on any review date on the basis of demonstrably superior performance.

4. Salaries determined and paid by the University under the provisions of paragraph 2 and 3 above shall be at the sole discretion of the employer and shall not be the subject of grievances.

Twelve (12) Hour Shifts

1. It is agreed that twelve (12) hour shift schedules will be arranged in such a manner so that F.P.O.'s will normally work 3 x 12 hour shifts on days, have 3 days off and work 3 x 12 hour shifts on nights. It is understood that this normal shift scheduling will not result in overtime payments.

2. To average the hours worked in a six (6) week cycle to 40 hours per week, the employer will schedule one (1) 12 hour shift off per F.P.O., for each 6 week cycle worked. This will be known as a rotation day. In the event of scheduling difficulties, unused rotation days will be compen-

sated for by cash payment at the regular rate at the mutual agreement between the employee and the employer.

3. Articles 14.02(a), 14.11, XVI, XVII, 19.01 and 19.03 refer to an 8 (eight) hour day unless stipulated as a calendar day. The intent is to ensure that no additional costs to the employer are generated in these or any other sections of the collective agreement as a result of this arrangement.

4. Note: For clarification of paid holidays, it is understood that an employee who does not work on a paid holiday will receive 8 (eight) hours straight time pay. An employee who works on a paid holiday will receive 2 x his or her normal rate for all hours worked plus an additional 8 (eight) hours statutory holiday pay.

(B) Shift Premiums

Shifts starting between 1200 hours (noon) and 1800 hours shall carry a premium of thirty cents ($.30) per hour.

Shifts starting between 1800 hours and 0600 hours the next day shall carry a premium of fifty-five cents ($.55) per hour.

Shifts in which more than fifty per cent (50%) of the time worked falls on Saturday shall carry a premium of twenty-five cents ($.25) per hour.

Shifts in which more than fifty per cent (50%) of the time worked falls on Sunday shall carry a premium of fifty-five cents ($.55) per hour.

The premiums shall not be paid where the time worked is paid at the overtime rate.

Example 2

Wage Rate Schedule

(Effective January 5, 1987)

JOB CLASSIFICATION	RATE
Student Employee Rates for period April 15 to Sept. 30	
Group 1	
Select and Packer	$11.94
Group 1(a)	
Carton Assembly Labourer	12.09
Empty Tray Stacker	12.09

Group 2
General Labourer	12.29
First Aid Attendant 'B'	12.29

Group 3
Sweeper Operator	12.39
First Aid Attendant 'A'	12.39

JOB CLASSIFICATION

Regular Employee Rates

	Start	3 months	6 months
Group 1			
Select and Packer	$11.94	13.79	13.94
Group 1(a)			
Carton Assembly Labourer	12.09	13.94	14.09
Empty Tray Stacker	12.09	13.94	14.09
Group 2			
General Labourer	12.29	14.19	14.29
First Aid Attendant 'B'	12.29	14.19	14.29
Group 3			
Sweeper Operator	12.39	14.29	14.39
First Aid Attendant 'A'	12.39	14.29	14.39
Group 4			
Forming Cleaner		14.29	14.49
Mould Handler		14.29	14.49
Hand Palletizer		14.29	14.49
Group 4(a)			
Auto Palletizer		14.39	14.59
Group 5			
Lift Truck Operator		14.62	14.77
Mould Cleaner		14.59	14.74
Group 5(a)			
L.T.O. Checker		14.77	14.82
Group 6			
Carton Assembly Attendant	14.72	14.78	14.84
Warehouse Attendant	14.75	14.81	14.87

Payloader-Truck Driver	14.72	14.78	14.84
Labelling Cleaner (floater)	14.72	14.78	14.84

Group 7

Oiler	14.80	14.86	14.94
Batchperson	14.80	14.86	14.94
Mould Polisher/Welder	14.80	14.86	14.94
I.S. Machine Helper	14.80	14.86	14.94

Group 8

Maintenance Assistant	14.59	14.74	15.04
Lehr & Instrument Assistant	14.59	14.74	15.04
Ware Inspector	14.90	14.97	15.04
Equipment Inspector (cat & backhoe)	14.90	14.97	15.04
Stores Attendant	14.90	14.97	15.04

Group 9

Day Inspector	14.99	15.11	15.24
Batch & Tank Lab. Tech.	14.99	15.11	15.24

Group 10

I.S. Machine Operator	15.04	15.19	15.59
Furnace Attendant	15.04	15.19	15.59
Upkeep Attendant	15.04	15.19	15.59
Labelling Operator	15.04	15.19	15.59

Group 11

Maintenance Person (non-certified)	15.49	15.69	15.89
Mould Maker (non certified)	15.49	15.69	15.89
Shift Technician (non certified)	15.49	15.69	15.89

Group 11(a)

Power House Attendant	16.24	16.44	16.64

Group 12

Workout Person	16.34	16.44	16.79

Group 13
B.C. Certified Journeyperson

Tradesperson	17.74	18.14	

Example 3

Appendix "A"

Salary Schedule
Effective January 1985

CLASSIFICATION	JAN. 1, 1985
Matron	$ 9.73

CODE 1

Caretaker Start	10.47
Caretaker after 1 year	11.07
Caretaker with 4th class certificate	11.35
Caretaker with 3rd class certificate	11.43

CODE 2

Shift Leader other than on days	11.35
with 4th class certificate	11.63
with 3rd class certificate	11.71

CODE 3

Shift Leader Days	11.47
with 4th class certificate	11.74
with 3rd class certificate	11.82

CODE 4

Head Caretaker Public School "C" (up to & including 14 rooms)	12.58
with 4th class certificate	12.87
with 3rd class certificate	12.93

CODE 5

Head Caretaker Public School "B" (15 rooms & up to & including 25 rooms)	12.72
with 4th class certificate	12.98
with 3rd class certificate	13.08

CODE 6

Head Caretaker Public School "A" (26 rooms and over)	12.81
with 4th class certificate	13.11
with 3rd class certificate	13.16

CODE 6A
Head Caretaker
   (School X & Y 15 cents per hour more)   12.96
with 4th class certificate   13.26
with 3rd class certificate   13.31

CODE 7
Head Caretaker Junior High School   12.97
with 4th class certificate   13.28
with 3rd class certificate   13.34

CODE 8
Head Caretaker Secondary School "B"
   (up to & including 1,599 students)   13.14
with 4th class certificate   13.42
with 3rd class certificate   13.51

CODE 9
Head Caretaker Secondary School "A"
   (1,600 students and over)   13.28
with 4th class certificate   13.56
with 3rd class certificate   13.64

CODE 9A
Head Caretaker at M.C.I. & J.H.S.   13.64
with 4th class certificate   13.92
with 3rd class certificate   14.01
Temporary Staff   6.58

SHIFT PREMIUM 40 CENTS PER HOUR

Note No. 1

   Code 8 Secondary Schools "B" shall be known as those schools with an enrolment below 1,600 pupils.

Note No. 2

   Code 9 Secondary Schools "A" shall be known as those schools with an enrolment above 1,600 pupils. Also to include the Education Administration Centre.

Note No. 3

   In the event that the category of a school drops in Code size to a lower Code, the Head Caretaker's wage rate will be correspondingly changed to the range for the lower Code. Conversely, if a school category increases to a higher Code, the Head Caretaker's wage rate will be changed to the corresponding rate for the higher Code. Any wage rate reclassification arising from a change in category size will become effective on the 30th September of each year as per the enrolment report from the Planning Department. The foregoing to apply to both Public and Secondary Schools.

Note No. 4

Any increment increase for Assistant Caretakers will become effective on the commencement of the payment period nearest the employee's anniversary date.

Note No. 5

As in past practice retroactivity to 1st January, 1985 in respect of wage and shift premium rates and overtime as denoted in Schedule "A". Retroactivity will apply to all employees on staff at the date of ratification, to employees who retired in 1985, prior to ratification and to the estate of an employee who died in 1985, prior to ratification.

3. Cost of Living

In the past few years, some negotiating parties have directed much collective bargaining attention and time to cost-of-living formulas. Since a number of collective agreements contain such a provision, a brief look at some of the variations on the cost-of-living formula is useful.

The basic theory of a cost-of-living provision in a collective agreement is that an employee's wages should increase in relationship to the overall cost-of-living in the community at large. In a period of inflation, the cost of commodities and services that we all purchase goes up. Expressed differently, the cost of maintaining one's normal lifestyle increases. While this is a statistical fact, it is also a generalization in that no one person's cost-of-living goes up in the same precise amount and degree as does another person's living costs, since we all live and buy differently. However, the federal government publishes figures which measure the impact, in average terms, of the general rise in the cost of some of the goods and services across the country and by region.

In collective bargaining terms, a cost-of-living formula is normally expressed as an addition to the direct wage increases that are negotiated. A wage increase may be expressed in percentage terms, or as so many cents per hour to be added to the current wage rates. Such a figure may be costed and applied under the terms of the collective agreement as required. The cost-of-living formula should be set out with care and precision, but the actual cost of the application of that formula is a matter of speculation since it depends upon a then unknown quantity, namely, the amount of increase in the cost-of-living during the period of time while the collective agreement operates.

The first matter for the parties, assuming there is no existing cost-of-living formula in their current collective agreement, is to agree on what will be the base against which future increases will be measured. Most collective agreements now use the 1971 base published by Statistics Canada as the starting point of reference. Once the base has been agreed upon, a factor must be applied to the increase in the base figure over the chosen time period, so that the difference can be translated into wage payments. The most common method of computation is that one or more cents per hour is paid for each point rise in the cost-of-living or specified portion of each such point. Two examples are as follows:

Example 1

(a) **This C.O.L.A. clause will take effect in the second year of the Agreement on the following basis:**

(b) **The chart will be 1971 = 100. The basis of payment will be .375 C.P.I. increase equals one cent ($.01) per hour increase in C.O.L.A. payment.**

(c) **The base figure for the beginning of C.O.L.A. will be the C.P.I. February 1986 figure. Payment, if any, will begin on May 1, 1986 and will be adjusted quarterly thereafter up to January 31, 1988. A partial payment may be made on January 31, 1988 but no further adjustment in C.O.L.A. will be made after that date.**

(d) **The maximum amount that can accrue under this C.O.L.A. clause is two dollars ($2.00) per hour.**

(e) **The C.O.L.A. payment will be paid on a per hour basis for all hours worked, but it will not be rolled into the regular hourly rate.**

Example 2

.01 First Year of the Agreement

For this purpose:

(a) **"The Consumer Price Index" means the Consumer Price Index for Canada as published by Statistics Canada (1971 = 100) and hereinafter called the "C.P.I."**

(b) **The base index means the C.P.I. for the month of February 1986 + 5%.**

(c) **The Cost of Living Allowance Program shall provide $0.01 per hour for each full .35 rise in the C.P.I. over the base index. Payments if any, will commence in the first pay period beginning in the month following the publication of the C.P.I. for May 1986 based on the total point advance in the May 1986 C.P.I. over the base index. Thereafter, the allowance will be adjusted upwards or downwards as required** at three (3) month intervals based on the index as of August 1986, November 1986 and February 1987.

(d) This allowance will be paid only on regular hours actually worked and shall not be considered for the purpose of computing overtime, premium time or any other earnings for any benefits based on wages unless otherwise required by law.

(e) No adjustment retroactive or otherwise shall be made due to any revision which may later be made in the published index.

(f) The continuance of the Cost of Living Allowance shall be contingent upon the availability of the official monthly C.P.I. in its present form and calculated on the same basis as the index in effect at the date of signing this agreement unless otherwise agreed by the parties.

.02 Second Year of the Agreement

For this purpose:

(a) "The Consumer Price Index" means the Consumer Price Index for Canada as published by Statistics Canada (1971 = 100) and hereinafter called the "C.P.I."

(b) The base index means the C.P.I. for the month of February 1987 + 5%.

(c) The Cost of Living Allowance Program shall provide $0.01 per hour for each full .35 rise in the C.P.I. over the base index. Payments if any, will commence in the first pay period beginning in the month following the publication of the C.P.I. for May 1987 based on the total point advance in the May 1987 C.P.I. over the base index. Thereafter, the allowance will be adjusted upwards or downwards as required at three (3) month intervals based on the index as of August 1987, November 1987 and February 1988.

(d) This allowance will be paid only on regular hours actually worked and shall not be considered for the purpose of computing overtime, premium time or any other earnings for any benefits based on wages unless otherwise required by law.

(e) No adjustment retroactive or otherwise shall be made due to any revision which may later be made in the published index.

(f) The continuance of the Cost of Living Allowance shall be contingent upon the advancement of the official monthly C.P.I. in its present form and calculated on the same basis as the index in effect at the date of signing this agreement unless otherwise agreed by the parties.

As stated in this example, the time period normally chosen for each calculation and adjustment is each quarter during the term of the collective agreement.

An important consideration is whether the increases generated by the application of the cost-of-living formula are to be paid to the employees as an "add-on", or are to be folded into the hourly wage rate and, if so, at what point in time. If the particular collective agreement results in a cost-of-living calculation of 20¢ per hour to be paid to the employees at the end of the relevant quarter, the collective agreement should be clear as to whether that sum is to be added onto the regular hourly wage rates or paid to the employees separately for each and every hour worked from that point forward. The importance of the issue is evident when one considers that the 20¢ per hour, if added to the wage rate, would result in a compounding or impacting effect for premium pay purposes where overtime is involved and vacations, paid holidays and other wage-related benefits are provided. If the increases are not added into the wage rate and particularly if the collective agreement is for a lengthy period of time, the parties will still have to negotiate a renewal of the collective agreement. At that time they will have to deal with what may be a considerable amount of money now being paid to each employee for each hour worked as a result of the application of the cost-of-living formula. The difficult negotiating question will be whether all or a portion of that sum of money should first be added to the then existing wage rates before further general wage increases are negotiated to cover the period of the new collective agreement.

There are other variations in the basic cost-of-living formula dealt with in some collective agreements. Some collective agreements provide a "trigger", which means that the cost-of-living calculated on whatever base figure is used must rise to a predetermined level before any cost-of-living payments are required. For instance, the collective agreement may provide that the cost-of-living over the appropriate time period must rise by at least one full point and the calculation will take into account only the amount of increase in excess of one point.

Another concept that may be built into the cost-of-living formula is a "cap". One of the difficulties that faces an employer who agrees to a cost-of-living arrangement is that it is open-ended in the sense that the employer can only guess as to the ultimate cost of what has been bargained, since economic forecasting is such a dismal science. Because the cost-of-living formula is both prospective and speculative, the employer cannot tell what the future wage rates will be as the term of the collective agreement unfolds and the wage rates will be increased in relationship to an unknown figure. One solution is that the parties agree on a maximum increase to be paid, notwithstanding the fact that the cost-of-living may escalate or increase beyond this pre-set figure.

One further observation should be made with respect to the application of a cost-of-living formula. As stated, the general purpose of a cost-of-living formula is to provide that wage increases of employees will rise in relationship to increases in the general cost-of-living. One practical problem is that the most frequently used cost-of-living formula benefits lower paid employees more than higher paid employees on a statistical basis. To make the point clear, assume that the cost-of-living formula results in a 30¢ per hour increase over a year. If the employee in question is paid $6 an hour, the amount of increase as a percentage of the wage rate is significantly more than if the employee is paid $10 per hour. To that degree, the logic of the concept that the purchasing power of each employee's wages should be maintained to the same degree as the cost-of-living increases is distorted between employees at different wage levels.

4. Job Descriptions

The important distinction between a job description and a job title has already been explained. A number of collective agreements go beyond the specification of job titles and include job descriptions for some or all of the jobs performed by employees in the bargaining unit. Many employers regard the creation and implementation of job descriptions as being solely the prerogative of management, and have refused to agree to negotiate job descriptions at the bargaining table. Some unions are content to let the employer have the right to decide on the content of jobs, but agree that the corresponding responsibility of the union is to negotiate an appropriate wage rate for each of the jobs. In other words, these unions are not concerned with negotiating job descriptions but only with the rates for the jobs.

There are other unions that regard the subject of job descriptions as of critical importance to their members. In that event, the employer must decide how hard to fight on this issue. As always, once they agree, the parties may describe the jobs with whatever descriptive words they choose and with as much detail as they wish.

A few collective agreements go beyond the reciting of the different job descriptions to set out each of the elements of the job for the purpose of specifying not only the proper functions of the job but also the method by which each job should be ranked in the wage schedule in relation to other jobs. One example of this approach is the Co-operative Wage Study of the United Steelworkers of America. If the employer and the union agree in their negotiations to a CWS program, each job in the employer's operation is broken down into a number of constituent elements in accordance with the CWS manual. Each of the elements is factored and added together and the total number of points determines the wage level. Thus, there may be fifteen or twenty pay levels under such a collective bargaining arrangement with a given wage differential between each level. Individual jobs are slotted at the proper pay level as required. If the job content changes, the job is refactored and may be moved up or down in the pay scale depending on the degree of change.

5. Shift Differentials

The final matter to be discussed under the heading of wages is shift differentials. If the operation has only one work shift, there is no need to establish a differential to be paid to employees on some other shift. However, in a number of operations, employees work on a second or third shift and many collective agreements provide for an additional premium amount over and above the basic wage rate for these employees.

The general principle of a shift differential is to compensate an employee who is required to work hours regarded as abnormal in the sense that they are outside "normal" day work hours. The amount of the shift differential is, of course, a subject to be considered as part of the economic package.

Once the actual amount is agreed upon, the parties must specify the group of employees entitled to the particular differential. This in turn requires precise language to avoid difficulties in the future in the interpretation of the collective agreement. For example, if the collective agreement provides that a shift premium is to be paid to all employees who work any hours between 4:00 p.m. and midnight, is the premium to be paid to an employee who worked his or her scheduled day shift, which ends at midnight, and also worked two hours of overtime from 12:00 a.m. to 2:00 a.m.? If the differential is intended to be paid only to employees who work a regularly assigned shift from 4:00 p.m. to midnight, the collective agreement should so state. Similarly, the parties must be careful to use language to clarify whether the shift differential is added to the wage rate and can be compounded or pyramided for overtime pay purposes.

Chapter 12

Vacations, Holidays and Other Time Outs

1. Vacations with Pay

Most collective agreements provide for the granting of vacations with pay, with the duration of the vacation and the amount of vacation pay based upon the length of service of each employee. The greater the length of service, the more vacation time off and vacation pay the employee receives.

Under the vacation with pay article, two quite separate issues must be covered. The first deals with the length of the employee's vacation period and the second concerns the amount of vacation pay. In most jurisdictions, legislation establishes minimum vacation entitlements which by and large require that employees who have at least one year of service are entitled to two weeks' vacation with pay. Most collective agreements provide additional vacation benefits to employees who have extended years of service. For instance, employees with five years of service may be entitled under the relevant collective agreement to three weeks' vacation, and employees with, say, fifteen years of service may be entitled to four weeks' vacation.

As a matter of law, the provisions of the collective agreement must provide as a minimum the statutory vacation benefits, and the parties may not contract out of the rights and obligations set out in the statute. Thus, in the unlikely event the parties are prepared to agree to a provision which grants less than the statutory minimum, the legislation supersedes the collective agreement and the vacation article will be deemed to be amended to the extent that there is a shortfall. The converse of this is that the statutory schemes establish a negotiating floor, not a ceiling. As a result, the parties to a collective agreement are free to negotiate any vacation provisions they choose beyond what the legislation provides.

While the concept is by no means common, a few collective agreements provide for special vacation allowances in given circumstances. For instance, the collective agreement may provide that employees who have a particular length of service may become entitled on a periodic basis, for example, every five years, to an additional period of vacation over and above the standard amount of vacation entitlement. In a sense, such an arrangement is a partial industrial equivalent to the sabbatical leave of absence in the academic world.

A further matter that must be considered by the parties is the question of the point in time when the entitlement to a specific vacation becomes vested or determined. If the employees become entitled to vacations on the basis of a schedule of length of service, does the entitlement commence on the individual employee's anniversary date or on a common date applied to all employees? If the former, it means that vacation entitlements are individual and become operative throughout the calendar year as different employees pass through the anniversary date of their employment. This system can create administrative difficulties and as a result many parties to collective agreements specify a date in the year, frequently June 30, on which the amount of each employee's vacation is determined or calculated for that year. Put simply, this means that on June 30, if that is the date chosen, the employer would review the service date of all employees in the bargaining unit and the individual vacation entitlement would be determined by each employee's service on June 30.

Once the amount of vacation time to be taken has been decided by the negotiating parties, consideration must be given to when and by whom vacations will be scheduled. On this issue there is a wide variation in the practice under different collective agreements. In some cases the plant or operation may have an annual shutdown period during which no bargaining unit employees will be scheduled to work. If this is the case, and especially if the shutdown period is at least two weeks, it is a simple matter to schedule the bulk of the vacations of the employees for that period of time. If a newly hired employee under the collective agreement is entitled to one week of vacation, the second week would be treated as an authorized leave of absence without pay. If the employee in question is entitled to a vacation of longer than two weeks, the third, fourth, or fifth week of vacation would be scheduled at some other time in the year.

There are many other operations which do not have an annual shutdown period or, if there is one, the employer may require some employees to perform work during the shutdown period. In these cases, the scheduling of the vacation becomes a matter of some difficulty, since many employees prefer to have their vacation during the summer months to coincide with school breaks and the availability of their families.

In some collective agreements, the employer has the right to determine when the vacation is to be taken. Typical language would read, "at a time convenient to the employer". Other collective agreements provide for the scheduling of vacations on a preferential basis depending upon the length of service of employees. The more senior employees have the first choice of when their vacations will be taken. An example is:

Senior employees, in keeping with the efficient operations of the employer, shall be granted preference as to vacation time.

Even if such an arrangement is agreed between the parties, many employers will insist on the right to decide how many employees may be absent at any point in time. Since the more senior employees are likely to be in the more important jobs — important in the operational sense — the employer may well find it difficult to carry on normal operations if the employees decide for themselves when their own vacations will be taken. An example of a provision that tries to accommodate these respective interests is as follows:

Employees shall be required to take such vacation period to which they are entitled consistent with the company's ability to maintain an efficient operation. Vacation will be granted on the principle of seniority.

The company agrees to post the vacation schedule on March 31 of each year, and employees shall sign for their first choice for the vacation period.

In the first week of April employees displaced from their first choice shall have the right to choose an alternate period.

After the first week of April, the vacation schedule shall be frozen, and no employee shall be displaced from the vacation period to which they have been assigned without the approval of the employee concerned and the company.

Vacations of multiple weeks lead to the splitting up of vacations into separate blocks of time. If an employee under the collective agreement is entitled to five weeks of vacation, is he or she entitled to take all five weeks consecutively, or is the period of vacation to be split up and, if so, on what basis? What about unused vacations from last year? Because of the need for the employer to have at work a complement of employees who can perform the necessary jobs, many collective agreements provide that the employer may require the employees to take their vacations by a certain date and do not permit unused vacation time being rolled into the next vacation year. An example of such a clause is as follows:

Vacations must be taken by all employees entitled thereto and must be completed by March 31 and cannot accumulate or be taken in subsequent vacation years.

A further observation concerning the scheduling of vacations is that many parties to collective agreements have administrative practices they have found to be mutually satisfactory which may or may not be addressed in their collective agreement. For example, the employer may post a notice to employees in the plant directing them to list their preferred vacation dates.

The employer may then try and match the preferred dates of the individual employees with the need to maintain at all times a workforce that can keep the operations going. Further, the parties may have an arrangement that the vacation schedule is to be announced to the employees on a date well before the beginning of the vacation period itself. A not uncommon date to post vacation schedules is April 1. The purpose of this posting is obviously to provide advance notice to the employees of when their vacations are scheduled so that they can make their own plans.

Apart from the general notion of vacation pay, one matter that concerns both parties is the basis of calculation of the pay. In Ontario, the *Employment Standards Act* provides a minimum vacation pay entitlement which is 4% of the total earnings of employees with more than one year of service. Many collective agreements accept this principle and provide for vacation pay on a percentage basis which, generally speaking, is expressed through a formula of 2% for each week of vacation. If an employee is entitled to three weeks of vacation, that person would be entitled to 6% of total earnings as vacation pay.

There are two things that should be discussed concerning the use of a percentage calculation for vacation pay purposes. In the first place, the parties must be careful to designate what they mean by "total earnings". Does this sum include the vacation pay for the preceding year? Does it include amounts paid to employees by virtue of the operation of a weekly indemnity policy under the same collective agreement? Does it include payments to employees by operation of a statute such as the *Workers' Compensation Act*? An example of a definition of total earnings for vacation pay purposes taken from one collective agreement is as follows:

> **Total earnings shall mean wages received from the employer as taxable income during the twelve (12) month period ending June 30 prior to the vacation period but exclusive of any vacation pay.**

Another approach is to state that total earnings shall include the defined elements in the appropriate legislation, for example, "wages" as defined in section 1 of the Ontario *Employment Standards Act* during the previous year. That definition reads:

(*p*) "wages" means any monetary remuneration payable by an employer to an employee under the terms of a contract of employment, oral or written, express or implied, any payment to be made by an employer to an employee under this Act, and any allowances for room or board as prescribed in the regulations or under an agreement or arrangement therefor but does not include,

   (i) tips and other gratuities,

(ii) any sums paid as gifts or bonuses that are dependent on the discretion of the employer and are not related to hours, production or efficiency,

(iii) travelling allowances or expenses,

(iv) contributions made by an employer to a fund, plan or arrangement to which Part X of this Act applies.

The second consideration concerns the concept of using a percentage calculation to determine vacation pay. Subject to the definition of earnings, if an employee has been off work for a significant period of time during the preceding vacation year, the gross earnings will have been reduced in relation to the loss of wages as a result of the absence. Thus, a percentage of the employee's earnings would produce an amount of vacation pay that is less than the normal wages or salary for the week or weeks of vacation to which the employee is entitled. Conversely, if the employee has worked steadily throughout the year, including a substantial number of overtime hours, a percentage of total earnings would produce an amount in excess of normal wages for the week or weeks in question. For this reason, some collective agreements provide that vacation pay will be calculated not on the basis of a percentage of earnings but on the basis of a normal day's or week's pay. If the employee is entitled to two weeks of vacation, the amount of vacation pay is two times a normal week's pay or salary.

Provided that the employee receives at least the minimum amount of vacation pay as stipulated in whatever legislation may apply, there is nothing to preclude the employer and the union from using a non-percentage method to establish the amount of vacation pay. For example, the clause may read as follows:

Each day of vacation taken by an employee will be paid at his or her current rate(s) for his or her normal working hours for that day. No premiums or bonuses will, however, apply.

Some collective agreements insert a clause which guarantees that in any event an employee will receive at least the vacation pay to which the person is entitled in accordance with the statute that applies to the employer's operation. In addition, the collective agreement may provide that the vacation pay will be calculated both on a percentage basis and on the basis of the employee's normal wage for the relevant period of time, and the employee will be paid the greater of these two amounts. An example of a complete vacation schedule that illustrates a number of points that have been discussed is as follows:

.01 The qualifying year for permanent employees shall be based on the

anniversary date of the employee. Anniversary Date is the date on which he or she last commenced employment with the company as a probationary and permanent employee. Eligibility for vacations shall be on the following basis:

Length of Service	Vacation Entitlement
After one (1) year	2 weeks
After three (3) years	3 weeks
After ten (10) years	4 weeks
After sixteen (16) years	4 weeks plus 1 day
After seventeen (17) years	4 weeks plus 2 days
After eighteen (18) years	4 weeks plus 3 days
After nineteen (19) years	4 weeks plus 4 days
After twenty (20) years	5 weeks

.02 Vacation pay for each week of vacation shall be at the rate of 2% of the gross annual earnings earned during the employee's anniversary year (exclusive of taxable benefits and vacations already paid) or current annual rate, whichever is the greater.

.03 An employee may apply to take his or her vacation entitlement in an unbroken period subject to Article .09. The minimum vacation which may be taken at any time is one (1) work week subject to the provisions of Article .08. Work week shall mean an individual's work week excepting lieu days as defined in Article ___, or statutory holidays. An employee with less than five (5) days of vacation entitlement remaining within his or her anniversary year shall take the remaining days in an unbroken period subject to Article .08.

.04 When a specified holiday falls within an authorized vacation period, one (1) additional day shall be granted continuous with the vacation period.

.05 Except with prior approval of the company, vacations must be taken within the twelve (12) month period following the anniversary date of the employee and shall not be accumulated. Employees may make written requests for approval to carry over vacation credits to the following year for reason of travel, etc. Such requests shall state the amount of vacation credits the employee wishes to carry over and the reason for the request.

.06 All submissions for vacation should be made in writing prior to March 1 for the following twelve (12) month period. These applications will be processed and approved subject to Article .09 and posted by April 1. These approvals cannot be changed without the consent of the affected employees.

Submissions received after March 1 must be made in writing at least two (2) months in advance of vacation and approvals will be posted one

(1) month in advance of vacation subject to operational requirements and Article .09.

.07 In the event of a conflict arising between two (2) or more employees as to when they take their vacation, the most senior employee shall have the preference.

.08 The employer shall attempt to provide vacations during the periods preferred by employees; however, in scheduling vacations, the employer shall ensure that operational requirements are met and that a sufficient number of personnel is available to provide the required level of service.

.09 An employee terminating employment at any time in the vacation year prior to using his or her vacation, shall be entitled to payment of wages in lieu of such vacation prior to termination, in accordance with Article .02.

2. Paid Holidays

Under most collective agreements, a number of specified holidays are listed and employees, perhaps with certain exceptions, are paid their normal day's pay even though they do not work on the holiday. While this appears to be a somewhat straightforward arrangement, a number of questions and considerations have to be examined by the negotiators.

To begin with, is the employee to be paid holiday pay when the holiday falls on a day on which the employee would not normally work, such as a Saturday or Sunday? At one time, many collective agreements provided that holiday pay would be paid only when the holiday fell on what would otherwise be a normal working day. The reasoning was that the employee should receive a full week's pay, even though less than a complete week was worked because of the intervention of the holiday. On the other hand, if the holiday fell on a non-working day, holiday pay would not be paid since the employee would have received normal wages for the normal week that was worked. As time went on, it became more common for holiday pay to be paid regardless of the day of the week on which the holiday fell, the argument being that the employee had earned both the day off work and the pay by the time the holiday arrived. In short, this is an "earned" benefit that is paid automatically in contrast to a "purposeful" benefit that is paid to achieve a purpose, in this case that an employee will not receive less than a normal week's pay even though less than a week is worked because of the holiday.

To some degree, there is a necessary division of holidays into those celebrated on a specific calendar date, such as Christmas Day, and those that occur on a proclaimed date, such as Victoria Day. The latter, by operation of statute, falls on a Monday which is a normal working day for most employees. However, the practice under some collective agreements has been for other holidays which fall on a non-working day such as a Saturday or Sunday to be celebrated for purposes of the collective agreement on a regular working day that is designated by the employer. Other collective agreements provide that the employer has the option of designating some other day for the celebration of the holiday or to pay the employee for the holiday as though it had fallen on a regular working day. An example of this kind of provision is as follows:

> **The following plant holidays, regardless of when they fall, will be granted with pay to all employees who have completed their probationary period:**

New Year's Day	**Labour Day**
Good Friday	**Thanksgiving Day**
Victoria Day	**Christmas Day**
Dominion Day	**Boxing Day**
Civic Holiday	**Two (2) Floating Holidays**

> **Payments for such holidays shall be based on the employee's regular hourly rate multiplied by the number of hours he or she would normally have worked on such day. When any of the said holidays falls on other than a regular working day, then the employer may either designate some other day as the day upon which the said holiday will be celebrated, or pay the employees who qualify for payment for the said holiday as though it had fallen on a regular working day, whichever the employer prefers.**

It will be noted from this example that the employees who are entitled to pay for the holidays are those who have completed their probationary period. Many collective agreements provide that payment for holidays is granted to all employees, including those who have not yet attained seniority.

In addition, there are a number of other variations on the formula for calculating the amount of holiday pay. The most common approach is to ensure that the employee will be paid a normal day's pay, and for this purpose the person is treated as being at work for the normal complement of hours for the day. This can create problems between various employees who may be entitled to some form of premium pay based, for example, on the shift premium they would have worked but for the holiday. Thus, one employee would receive more money for the paid holiday than another in that the shift employee would be paid a normal day's pay plus the premium for the shift that would have been worked. While there is nothing inherently wrong with the idea of paying different amounts of holiday pay to different employees, it can cause friction. For this reason it is important that the parties be clear in expressing what different groups of employees are going to receive. Provision should also be made for the employee who works on a paid holiday. Under many collective agreements, the employee receives holiday pay and is also paid premium pay for the hours actually worked on the holiday. An example of such a provision would read:

If an employee works on one (1) of the above named plant holidays, he or she shall receive payment at time and one-half (1½) for the hours actually worked by him or her in addition to receiving his or her holiday pay.

In the public sector some collective agreements provide that an employee who works on a paid holiday will receive holiday pay plus pay for the hours worked or additional time off with pay to be taken at a later date. An example of such an approach is as follows:

An employee required to work on any of the foregoing holidays shall be paid at the rate of two (2) times his or her regular hourly rate for time worked on such holiday in addition to any holiday pay to which the employee may be entitled. At the option of the employer the employee may be granted an equivalent amount of time off in lieu of the holiday pay. The employee may request such equivalent time off and the employer will use its best endeavours to grant it in accordance with the employee's wishes.

A further matter that may be dealt with by the parties concerns a paid holiday which takes place while an employee is on vacation. Many collective agreements stipulate that when this occurs, the employee is to be given an additional day's vacation with pay. Other collective agreements provide the option of an entire day's pay or an additional day off with pay. For instance, the provision might read:

If one (1) of the above holidays covered by paragraph ___ of Article ___ occurs within an employee's vacation period the employee may elect either of the following:

(a) To receive eight (8) hours' pay at his or her regular rate for such paid holiday in addition to his or her vacation pay,

OR

(b) Elect to take an additional day off with pay at a time mutually agreed between the company and the employee. If no suitable agreement can be reached between the parties the final decision shall be determined by local management. If the employee wishes to make an election as provided for in Clause ___ hereof, he or she shall advise the company

of such election within a reasonable time prior to the vacation period assigned to, or chosen by him or her.

One matter that is of importance, not only in the negotiations but also in administrating the language of the article, is the condition under which an employee who is absent from work for a period of time before or after the holiday loses entitlement to holiday pay. The employee may wish to extend a long weekend by staying away on either the day before the holiday or the day after the holiday. Another example would be a situation where an employee is on lay-off at the time the holiday occurs or is receiving workers' compensation.

With respect to the former, many collective agreements have built-in language to protect against abuse in relation to payment for holidays. The most common approach is that the employee must work the full working day both before and after the holiday, or else become disentitled to holiday pay. Many collective agreements modify this requirement to the extent that the employee must work the day before and after the paid holiday "unless absent with the permission of the employer" or "unless absent due to illness or other reasonable cause".

The right to receive holiday pay while on a lay-off is less commonly dealt with under collective agreements. However, it is an area that has caused disputes and grievances, and it is one subject to which more attention should be given by negotiating parties. If the lay-off is of long duration and a holiday occurs in the middle of the lay-off, most employers will argue that the employee should not receive holiday pay because the employee has not worked in some time, perhaps many months. If a short-term lay-off takes place immediately before the holiday and the employee returns to work a few days later, the union may argue that the rights of the employees can be abused by the employer timing the lay-off to avoid paying for the holiday. One example of a provision that addresses these concerns is as follows:

.01 (a) To qualify for holiday pay, an employee must do the following:

(i) Complete the probationary period;

(ii) Work the scheduled work day immediately preceding and work the scheduled work day immediately succeeding the holiday. However, an employee absent the day before or after a holiday will receive holiday pay provided an excuse is acceptable to the employer.

(b) Employees on lay-off for ten (10) calendar days or less, immediately preceding or including a paid holiday will be paid for such holiday.

.02 The pay shall be calculated for a holiday on the basis of eight (8)

hours times the regular straight time, including premium pay. Holidays whose significance is not necessarily associated with a given day may be celebrated by the employer at the beginning or end of the work week at its discretion. This is done in the interest of providing a maximum of production and the maximum time off for employees. An employee, who has agreed to work on any holiday and does not work said day, shall receive no pay for this holiday, unless an excuse is given which is acceptable to the employer.

3. Leaves of Absence

It may be felt that the subject of leaves of absence is not properly an economic issue. However, in a general sense, the circumstances and terms under which leaves of absence may be granted have cost implications for the employer and as a result it will be discussed in this chapter.

The situations under which a leave of absence may be sought are many, but for collective bargaining purposes there are at least the following categories:

(a) **leave of absence for personal reasons;**

(b) **leave of absence for maternity purposes or, more recently, paternity or adoption;**

(c) **leave of absence for union purposes;**

(d) **bereavement leave of absence;**

(e) **leave of absence for jury duty; and**

(f) **educational leave of absence.**

(a) For personal reasons

Collective agreements include a wide variety of articles concerning the granting of a leave of absence for personal reasons. Under some collective agreements, there are restrictions on the length of time for such a leave of absence, as well as on the number of employees who may be granted a leave of absence at the same time. Restrictions are also found in many collective agreements to the extent that the employer has a right to refuse a request for leave of absence in certain specified circumstances. Differences may arise where the employee feels the request is justified but the employer feels the employee's job skills are needed during the period of the proposed absence. For this reason, the employer may be prepared to grant employees leave to be away for personal reasons but will want protective language such as the following:

The company will grant leave of absence without pay if an employee

requests it in writing and if the leave is for good reason and does not unreasonably interfere with the operation of the plant. Any such leave of absence shall not exceed seventy-five (75) calendar days.

(b) Maternity leave

The matter of maternity leave is dealt with in most jurisdictions by statute. Depending on which law applies, the employer in most cases will be bound by statute to grant pregnancy leave to an employee and to provide a job for the employee when she returns from pregnancy leave. The period of the pregnancy leave varies from province to province. In most instances, the employee must elect within a given number of months after the birth whether she wishes to return to work. The concept and many of the benefits of maternity leave are increasingly applied to circumstances of adoption and, as one of the very few examples of male catch-ups, to male employees who want paternity leave of absence.

(c) For union purposes

Most unions conduct periodic conferences and seminars for union members, stewards and committee members throughout the term of the collective agreement. One of the benefits of office in the union is the opportunity to attend such conferences which usually take place during the normal work week and, in some cases, at locations far from the place of employment. The union may want the contractual right to obtain leaves of absence so that employees can attend; the employer, on the other hand, may want to ensure that its operations are not unduly hampered by numbers of employees being absent at any one time. The employer may also want to be able to refuse to grant a particular employee's request for leave where the person is a key employee whose absence would seriously affect the running of the business. An article found in many collective agreements is as follows:

The employer will grant a leave of absence to an employee to attend union conventions and conferences provided that such leave does not interfere with the efficient operation of the plant. However, provided the employer receives two (2) weeks' notice from the union, this leave may be extended to three (3) employees, provided said leave will not affect production. The decision will be made at the discretion of the employer, and such permission shall not be unreasonably withheld.

(d) Bereavement leave

If an employee suffers a death in the immediate family, that person will undoubtedly want a leave of absence to grieve and take part in family observances. In contemplation that someone will be bereaved during the period of the collective agreement, most agreements provide for the granting of leave for a specified number of days and, unlike the other forms of leave of absence that have been discussed, may also provide that the employee will be paid a normal day's pay for each day of the period of absence. To avoid disputes as to its application, the article should provide a clear definition of the immediate family. There may be a difference in the number of days of leave of absence to be granted depending on the relationship between the deceased and the employee. As a general rule, the closer the relationship, the more likely it is the article will provide for a greater period of leave of absence than in the case of a distant relative. The collective agreement may also provide that the purpose of the granting of the leave of absence is for the employee to attend the funeral, to make arrangements for the burial, and to take part in the necessary family proceedings. This form of restrictive language may be required where there have been administrative difficulties and a sense that there has been abuse of the policy. A typical bereavement leave clause reads as follows:

When an employee is absent from work on a regular work day to attend the funeral of an immediate relative, he or she shall be paid for eight (8) hours at his or her regular rate of pay for each day of such absence up to a maximum of three (3) consecutive regular work days.

For the purpose of this clause, an immediate relative shall be defined as follows: Father, Father-in-law, Mother, Mother-in-law, Brother, Sister, Spouse, Grandparent, Grandchild, Son or Daughter.

When an employee is absent from work on a regular work day and loses pay to attend the funeral of a Brother-in-law, Sister-in-law, Son-in-law or Daughter-in-law, he or she shall be reimbursed at his or her regular rate of pay for his or her regular hours lost up to a maximum of eight (8) regular hours.

Where an employee is absent from work on a regular work day and loses pay to attend a memorial service for any of the aforementioned relatives, he or she shall be reimbursed at his or her regular rate of pay for his or her regular hours lost up to a maximum of eight (8) regular hours. The company may require from the employee proof of his or her attendance at such memorial service before it reimburses him or her hereunder.

Provisions of this article shall not apply to employees then receiving other company benefits such as vacation pay, sickness and accident payments or on an authorized leave of absence without pay for any reason.

An employee will not be entitled to receive under this Article ___ bereavement pay in respect of a day for which he or she is receiving holiday pay.

(e) Jury duty

As to the matter of jury duty, it may be anticipated under a collective agreement that certain of the employees covered will be asked to perform jury duty during the life of the agreement. While the employer would have no option but to grant a leave of absence, the question may arise as to whether the employee should be paid by the employer an amount equal to the difference between the amount paid for jury duty and the normal wages for the time in question. Under many collective agreements, this difference is made up by the employer so the employee does not suffer any economic loss while taking part in the functions of a jury. An example of a typical jury duty clause is as follows:

The employer will provide to all employees who have completed their probationary period and have been excused from work due to being subpoenaed for jury duty, a leave and allowance pay for the time spent on jury duty. This allowance pay will be calculated in the following manner. The employer agrees to pay the difference between the regular straight time wages for the scheduled time lost, which he or she would have otherwise worked, and a jury fee. This will be accomplished by the employee, upon receipt of his or her jury fee, endorsing it to the employer in exchange for the straight time hours allowance pay.

(f) Educational leave

The subject of educational leave can be considered from two different points of view. The first concept deals with an employee who wishes to take a program or course in an educational subject unrelated to his or her employment. Contractual provisions to deal with a leave of absence in such circumstances are comparatively rare and are usually dealt with under a general leave clause where leave is sought for personal reasons. The second notion is where the employer either wants the employee to upgrade his or her skills and knowledge or at least will benefit from the employee's attendance at a particular course of study. An example of this kind of provision is as follows:

If required by the employer, an employee shall be entitled to leave of absence with pay and without loss of seniority and benefits to write examinations to upgrade his or her employment qualifications.

Where employees are required by the employer to take courses to

upgrade or acquire new employment qualifications, the employer shall pay the full costs associated with the courses.

Subject to operational requirements, the employer will make every reasonable effort to grant requests for necessary changes to an employee's schedule to enable attendance at a recognized upgrading course or seminar related to employment with the employer.

Chapter 13

Hours of Work, Overtime and Other Benefits

1. Hours of Work

One of the provisions in a collective agreement that can generate the most administrative difficulties is one that defines the normal hours during which employees are scheduled to work. The reason is simple; there are few employment matters of more importance to employees than the hours they work. The contract language that lays out hours of work has two different dimensions: when the work is to be performed and what pay is to be received in return.

There are different ways to express the normal hours of work to be expected from employees. The working schedule may be set out as a number of hours per day or per week, or over some longer period of time such as a pay period. The hours may be expressed in numerical terms or they may be arranged in an itemized work schedule extending over a specific time. Another approach is to specify the starting and stopping time of each shift to be worked. Obviously, the determination of the appropriate language depends upon the particular operation that is being described and the needs of the parties.

Regardless of the language and form in which the hours of work are set out, some collective agreements begin this article with a clause which states that the hours of work as expressed in the collective agreement are not to be considered as a guarantee of hours of work. One provision reads as follows:

> **The following paragraphs and sections are intended to define the normal hours of work and shall not be construed as a guarantee of hours of work per day or per week, or of days of work per week.**

Next, the parties may set out a definition of what is to be considered a normal or standard work week. Assuming that the employees are not on a continuous shift operation — that is, one that operates regularly twenty-four hours a day, seven days a week — the standard work week would be expressed in terms of a five or six-day week. In the same clause there may be found a definition as to what constitutes a normal work day. Such a clause would read as follows:

The normal work week shall consist of forty (40) hours per week, comprised of five (5) eight (8) hour days.

Some collective agreements provide that a normal day or shift will commence at one specified time and end at another point in time. This is particularly the case where there are shifts which in turn must be defined. From an employer's point of view, it may be necessary to provide language that the normal shift times may be varied as required. An example of a clause which defines the normal shifts, and also sets out the circumstances when shifts may be changed, is as follows:

.02 With the exception of continuous shift operations, the normal work week shall consist of forty (40) hours comprised of five (5) eight (8) hour days, Monday to Friday, inclusive.

Normal shift times shall be as follows:

One and Two Shift Operations:

Day Shift	**7:00 a.m. to 3:30 p.m.**
Second Shift	**3:30 p.m. to 12:00 midnight**

Three Shift Operation:

Day Shift	**7:00 a.m. to 3:00 p.m.**
Second Shift	**3:00 p.m. to 11:00 p.m.**
Third Shift	**11:00 p.m. to 7:00 a.m.**

The Recording Receiver shall work the hours 7:30 a.m. to 4:30 p.m. with one (1) hour (unpaid) for lunch.

The company reserves the right to implement a shift at 12:00 noon to 8:00 p.m. as required. However, this shift shall be restricted to cover one (1) Storesperson.

The union shall be notified of the implementation of this shift not later than twenty-four (24) hours before the shift is put into operation.

.03 The normal work week in the case of continuous shift operations shall average forty-two (42) hours per week over a period of eight (8) weeks comprised of any six (6) consecutive eight (8) hour days.

The normal shift times for continuous shift operations shall be:

First Shift	**7:00 a.m. to 3:00 p.m.**
Second Shift	**3:00 p.m. to 11:00 p.m.**
Third Shift	**11:00 p.m. to 7:00 a.m.**

Continuous Shift is currently worked in the Plastics Department and the Kiln area of the Porcelain Department. The company agrees that this shall not be extended to other departments until it has been mutually agreed with the union.

Where shift operations are involved, the collective agreement may, and probably should, provide language detailing the manner in which employees rotate from one shift to another as well as the circumstances in which employees may be transferred in their shift assignments. The collective agreement may require the employer to pay an additional premium where an employee reports for work on a regularly assigned shift only to find that the shift hours have been changed without prior notice. This kind of provision recognizes that the employee may be required to move to different shift hours from those originally scheduled but, in return, a premium should be paid on the theory that the employee has been inconvenienced by the change being made without appropriate notice.

2. Overtime

Under most collective agreements, premium pay is paid for hours worked in excess of an employee's normal work schedule. While the amount of premium pay may vary depending on the number of hours that are worked, the compensation may be calculated on either a daily or weekly basis or both.

If overtime is expressed in terms of overtime hours worked on a daily basis, it follows that the employer would pay a premium for each hour worked by the employee beyond that employee's normal daily work schedule. A typical provision would read as follows:

Overtime at the rate of time and one-half ($1\frac{1}{2}$) the employee's regular hourly rate shall be paid for all work in excess of eight (8) hours per day.

It will be noted that this wording provides for premium pay of "all work" in excess of eight hours per day rather than "all hours" — a distinction that makes a large difference where the duration of the work is only a few minutes as distinct from sixty minutes or more.

Some collective agreements provide for an additional or extra premium to be applied to the hours in excess of a specified number of overtime hours worked on any particular day. For example, the collective agreement may provide for time and one-half as a premium payment for the first four hours of overtime worked, with additional hours of overtime to be paid at double pay.

Another way to express the employer's obligation to pay premium pay for overtime worked is in terms of a weekly computation. Under this arrangement, hours worked in excess of an employee's normal weekly work schedule will be paid at a premium rate. Assume an employee works four days in a row, each of which is a ten-hour day, and then is absent for the fifth day. Since the total number of hours worked in that week does not exceed forty, and even though the employee worked more than eight hours for the first four days in the week, overtime would not be paid for any hours worked during that week of work. As always there are compromises. In order to find a balance between the interests of the employer and the employee, the collective agreement could provide for a weekly overtime system. Where the employee has been absent during the week, he or she is obliged to work a number of additional hours in a given day before receiving overtime pay. For example, the first two hours might be paid at a regular rate of pay with the additional overtime hours paid at a premium rate.

If the operations are not regularly scheduled on a weekend, the collective agreement will normally provide some form of premium pay for work that is required on a Saturday or Sunday. The general pattern is that the premium amount is greater, usually double time, for work performed on Sunday. In industrial plants where maintenance work on machinery is performed on weekends when the production equipment is idle, an exception to the requirement to pay a premium for Saturday and Sunday work may be needed, in that both these days would be normally scheduled work days for maintenance employees who should be paid at the regular rate of pay for work performed on a Saturday or Sunday.

If shift employees are involved, particularly where the shifts operate on a continuous shift arrangement seven days per week, the overtime premium may be applied to hours worked on a scheduled day of rest. Thus, if the employee is required to work on a day on which he or she was scheduled not to work, regardless of the day in the week, overtime premium pay would be involved. Such a provision would read as follows:

Authorized overtime shall be paid for on the following basis:

(a) **Non-Continuous Shifts**

    (i) **Time and one-half (1½) for work performed up to four and one-half (4½) hours in excess of a normal work day.**

    (ii) **Time and one-half (1½) for work performed up to four and one-half (4½) hours on Saturday except where the work performed on Saturday is part of an employee's regularly scheduled shift.**

    (iii) **Double time for work performed in excess of four and one-half (4½) hours in excess of a normal work day.**

    (iv) **Double time for work performed in excess of four and one-half**

($4\frac{1}{2}$) hours on Saturday except where the work performed on Saturday is part of an employee's regularly scheduled shift.

(v) Double time for work performed on Sunday except where the work performed on Sunday is part of an employee's regularly scheduled shift.

(vi) Double time for work performed on a recognized holiday except where a regular shift overlaps the holiday.

(b) Continuous Shifts

(i) Time and one-half ($1\frac{1}{2}$) for work performed up to four and one-half ($4\frac{1}{2}$) hours in excess of a normal work day.

(ii) Time and one-half ($1\frac{1}{2}$) for work performed up to four and one-half ($4\frac{1}{2}$) hours on the first regularly scheduled day off or on the 6th consecutive day worked of a normal work week falling within one (1) pay period.

(iii) Double time for work performed in excess of four and one-half ($4\frac{1}{2}$) hours in excess of a normal work day.

(iv) Double time for work performed in excess of four and one-half ($4\frac{1}{2}$) hours on the first regularly scheduled day off or on the 6th consecutive day worked of a normal week falling within one (1) pay period.

(v) Double time for work performed on the second regularly scheduled day off.

(vi) Double time for work performed on a recognized holiday except where a regular shift overlaps the holiday.

Apart from the important issue of whether premium pay is to be computed at time and one-half or double time, the language should also answer the question of one and one-half times what amount. If the employee's wage rate under the collective agreement is expressed as an hourly rate, the agreement should state that the calculation is based upon the employee's regular hourly rate. If the employee is paid a salary, the collective agreement should set out the basis of conversion of the salary to an hourly rate for the purpose of calculating the appropriate premium payment for the hour that was worked. The collective agreement may also provide that overtime premiums should not be paid more than once. The purpose of this clause is to guard against the pyramiding of overtime. A typical clause reads as follows:

Overtime premiums shall not be paid more than once for any hour worked, and there shall be no pyramiding of overtime.

3. Rest Periods

During an employee's work day, rest periods are scheduled in accordance with the requirements of the collective agreement. The amount of time of a rest period will vary with the particular collective agreement although the most common is either a ten or fifteen-minute rest period during the first half of each shift and the same period during the second half. Invariably, this time is paid time in the sense that the employee's wages are not reduced and the time spent during the rest periods is treated as time worked even though in fact it has not been.

While some collective agreements specify the precise starting and finishing times for each rest period during a work day, most agreements provide flexibility for the scheduling of rest periods. This is particularly the case where there are large numbers of employees to be accommodated and where the operations cannot be shut down completely while employees take their breaks. A typical provision is as follows:

There shall be one (1) ten (10) minute rest period in the first half of each shift and one (1) ten (10) minute rest period in the second half of each shift to be granted at a time or times selected by the employer.

4. Reporting Time Pay

From time to time an employee reports for work on a regular working day with the expectation that regular work will be available only to find that some event has occurred and there is no work that day in his or her normal job. In these circumstances, many collective agreements provide that the employer is obliged to find other work for the employee to do or pay to the employee a specified number of hours of pay.

The reasoning for this form of provision is that the employee has been put to personal inconvenience by reporting for work at the usual starting time. Since the employer did not notify the employee not to report for work, particularly where there was an opportunity to do so, the employer should pay a form of penalty. While this may make sense on the basis that the employer should notify the employee, assuming that the employer can reasonably be expected to have known no work would be available, the logic is strained where the employee was not at work on the previous day or where the failure to provide work was caused by something beyond the employer's control, such as a fire or flood. In the result, the parties may provide an obligation for payment of reporting pay but add qualifying language so that payment need not be made where the employer was not at fault. This kind of clause reads as follows:

Any employee reporting for work without having been notified previously by the company not to report will be given a minimum of four (4) hours' work. If no work is available he or she will receive a minimum of four (4) hours' pay at his or her applicable wage classification rate if a non-incentive worker or in the case of a⁣ incentive worker his or her average rating factor will be applied. This provision will not apply when:

(a) Such a lack of work is due to fire, flood, power failure or some other cause clearly beyond the control of the company.

(b) The employee has failed to notify the company of his or her present address and telephone number on the forms supplied by the company.

5. Call-in Pay

Circumstances may arise in which an employee who has completed a regular shift of work and gone home is then contacted by the employer and directed to return to work. Most commonly, this kind of call would be made by the employer to a maintenance employee where there is a mechanical breakdown or emergency. The actual work that is performed may take only a short time, and yet the employee may have travelled some considerable distance to get to work and had his or her personal life interrupted by the call-in. In these circumstances, the collective agreement may provide for the payment of a minimum amount of wages to the employee, regardless of the time spent by the employee performing the work. A typical provision reads as follows:

An employee who has completed his or her regular shift and left the employer's premises and who is called back to perform work shall be paid a minimum of four (4) hours at time and one-half (1½) and be paid double time for all hours worked in excess of four (4).

6. Distribution of Overtime

The different ways to calculate premium pay for overtime hours that are worked have already been reviewed. What has not been considered is the right of an employee to refuse to work an assignment of overtime.

Depending on the wording of a particular collective agreement, overtime that is assigned to employees may be voluntary — that is, the assignment may be refused. In any event, the language should take into account the statutory provisions that deal with minimum and maximum hours of work in each jurisdiction. Generally speaking, overtime hours in excess of the maximum hours of work authorized by the statute, even though permitted to be assigned to employees, are not compulsory in the sense that an employee who does not want to work can be penalized for not working. However, the parties to a collective agreement may agree on language which sets out whether an employee must work an overtime assignment or in what circumstances it may be refused. Several examples follow:

Example 1

The company shall have the right to schedule overtime when, in its discretion, it is required. In the case of an individual employee the company will consider a reasonable request to be excused from overtime work on a particular occasion for a valid reason. The company agrees that when overtime work is required it will give as much notice thereof as practicable to the employees affected. The company further agrees that no disciplinary action will be taken against any employee because of his or her refusal to work overtime where less than twenty-four (24) hours notice is given to him or her that such overtime is required. The company agrees that except for employees in the Maintenance Department it will give at least twenty-four (24) hours notice of overtime which is regularly scheduled. Overtime will be equally distributed among the employees in their classification providing they are capable of doing the work.

Example 2

The employer shall give notice of overtime as far in advance as is practical. Opportunities for overtime work shall be distributed as equitably as practical among the employees normally performing the work and the acceptance of such overtime is voluntary. Once the employee has accepted the assignment, he or she has the responsibility to complete the assignment unless he or she has a valid reason for not so doing.

In the event the employer does not secure enough volunteers to perform the necessary work, then the employer may require the least senior qualified employee(s) to perform the work. The same employee will not be required to work overtime more than two (2) consecutive days. If overtime is required in the third day, the next senior qualified employee will be required to perform the work.

Apart from determining whether the overtime is voluntary, many collective agreements put restrictions on the right of the employer to assign overtime to any one person or group and protect against preference to one employee or group of employees in assigning overtime hours. Where a number of employees have the necessary qualifications to do the work involved, overtime may be assigned on some form of a rotating basis to ensure that over a period of time the overtime assignments are equalized, at least in part. This requirement as to which employee gets the overtime assignment deals with the opportunity to work overtime. If a given employee is unable or unwilling to work the overtime assignment, he or she is credited with the overtime hours that would have been worked for the purpose of comparing the overtime opportunities with those of other employees.

An example of a provision dealing with the distribution of overtime is as follows:

Overtime shall be distributed as equitably as possible amongst qualified employees in the department concerned.

The need for precision in the use of language in drafting collective agreements is illustrated by this clause. If the sentence were amended to read "distributed *equally* amongst employees in the department concerned", the effect would be substantially altered in two important respects. In the first place, there is a vital difference in meaning between the two words "equitably" and "equally", since the first deals with the notion of fairness and the latter is a precise mathematical computation. In the second place, removal of the word "qualified" would require that the total number of employees in the branch would be compared in relation to their overtime assignments rather than considering only the qualified employees.

7. Welfare Benefits

A typical collective agreement has provision for some form of employee welfare program. Some of the particular elements of the program could be hospital and medical coverage, sickness and accident indemnity, life insurance, superannuation and retirement compensation. While the benefits to be covered under any one collective agreement vary widely, some observations can be made that would apply to most collective agreements.

To begin with, there are two different ways to look at contractual obligations in respect of employee welfare plans. The first is a requirement to implement a specific plan that incorporates the individual benefits available for employees covered by the plan, and the second is to identify who is to pay the premium costs of the plan.

By virtue of the application of certain statutes, employers are obliged to make certain premium contributions towards the plans imposed by operation of law. One example would be workers' compensation premiums. However, employees may be obliged to pay some premiums towards coverage for certain plans such as provincial hospital coverage. The parties have no option as to whether these plans apply since they are imposed by statute. However, the parties may agree through their collective agreement that the employer will pay part or all of the employees' contribution towards the premium cost of the hospital benefits.

The parties may also want to provide medical and hospital coverage in excess of the basic benefits provided by provincial statute. In this situation, the parties would negotiate not only the specific supplementary medical and hospital coverage but also the question of who is to pay the premiums for the supplementary program.

Similarly, the parties could provide in their collective agreement for a group life insurance policy under which employees in the bargaining unit are insured for a specified amount of life insurance commonly expressed as an amount equal to some multiple of each employee's earnings. The employer may be obliged to implement a life insurance policy and continue the policy in full force and effect during the term of the collective agreement. Depending on the language used, the employer may also be required to keep the group life insurance policy with a named carrier, in contrast to a simple requirement that a policy to the designated coverage limit must be in effect while the collective agreement operates. If the employer is obliged to pay the full premium cost of the policy, it is more likely that a particular carrier will not be named, so the employer can obtain the most competitive rate available from the full range of insurance carriers. An example of a clause that does not specify the carrier is as follows:

The company shall continue to provide the corporate group medical, surgical, life insurance and pension plans during the life of this contract. These shall include:

— **100% of OHIP premiums**

— **life insurance @ one (1) times employee's previous year's earnings rounded to next higher $500.00**

— **A. & S. non-occupational insurance on a 1/4 basis for a maximum 26 weeks @ 60% of the employee's UIC insurable earnings with rebate used to provide benefits**

— **major medical including drugs on a 90/10 basis after a yearly deductible of $10.00 single and $20.00 family beginning January 1, 1982**

— **the existing pension plan**

— **dental plan @ 75% company paid and 25% employee paid**

Except for weekly indemnity benefits, the company shall continue to pay the premiums for all seniority employees for the month following the month of lay-off. Employees will pay their share of the dental plan.

The company or its insurers reserve the right to change any of the

above plans at any time providing the changes are not detrimental to employees.

UIC and CPP deductions will be made from weekly indemnity pay cheques. Weekly indemnity payments will be included in total earnings, applicable when calculating vacation pay.

With respect to sickness and accident indemnity plans, there are many variations but the most common is a program to enable the employee to receive a percentage of normal salary in the event of absence through sickness or accident for the period of such absence up to a maximum number of weeks. If the employee's absence results from an occurrence during the course of employment for which workers' compensation benefits are paid, normally, weekly indemnity benefits would not also be paid. In addition, the plan may provide for a waiting period of a number of days, especially in the event of absence through sickness.

While most weekly indemnity plans are the subject of a contract between the employer and an insurance company, there is nothing to stop the employer from financing the program itself, provided of course that the language of the collective agreement permits this form of self-insurance. Under this arrangement, the employer acts as its own insurer, and pays the benefits as required from its own pocket.

In the public sector, many collective agreements provide a sick pay program under which employees are credited with a specified number of days per month which are accumulated and which can be drawn upon by an employee who is absent through sickness. Effectively, what happens is that the employer establishes a bank of days of pay to draw upon so that when an absence occurs, an employee can be credited with the number of days in his or her sick leave bank without loss of pay. A typical sick leave plan of this kind reads as follows:

.01 Sick leave means the period of time an employee is permitted to be absent from work with full pay by virtue of being sick, quarantined or disabled, or because of an accident for which compensation is not payable under the *Workers' Compensation Act.*

.02 Permanent and probationary employees only, as covered by this agreement, shall accrue to their credit, one and one-half (1½) days per month of sick leave.

.03 Payment of benefits for accrued sick leave will be at the rate of 100% of an employee's daily pay.

.04 A deduction of one (1) day accumulated sick leave shall be made for each day benefit is paid.

.05 If benefits are receivable under the *Workers' Compensation Act*, an employee may choose, at the time of reporting the accident, to have such benefits increased to 100% of the employee's pay under Article .03 for which a deduction of one-quarter (1/4) day accumulated sick leave shall be made for each day's benefit paid, provided the employee has made proper notification to the employer, as outlined in the appropriate Departmental regulations.

.06 An employee who has completed five (5) years of service with the employer, upon termination of employment, he or she or his or her estate, shall be entitled to receive payment of one-half (1/2) the number of days to his or her credit at the rate of 100% of his or her latest daily rated pay. Maximum benefit to be one-half (1/2) year's salary.

.07 Time off during normal working hours may be paid from accrued sick leave credits for doctor or dentist appointments upon approval by the appropriate Superintendent. When requested the employee must provide a signed medical certificate, at the cost, if any, to the employer, confirming the appointment.

In considering contractual language that details such a program, the negotiator must deal with a number of different components. There must be provision for the establishment of accumulation of credits, as well as the manner in which the credits may be drawn against during the period of absence. There is also the question of what credits, if any, are to be paid to an employee on termination of employment or the retirement of the employee.

Pension benefits may flow from a clause or article of a collective agreement. On the other hand, the parties may negotiate a pension agreement setting out all of the terms and details of the pension plan in a separate agreement. The difficulty with this concept is that in law, there may only be one collective agreement in force at any point in time between an employer and a union. If the collective agreement has one term or duration and the pension agreement has a different term, confusion can arise as to which agreement governs when. For example, if the collective agreement has a term of two years and the pension agreement has a five-year term, can the union reopen negotiations on the pension plan on the expiry of the collective agreement? It could be argued that there can be only one collective agreement, and therefore the pension plan, notwithstanding it has three years to run, has expired along with the collective agreement. It is not possible to give an answer to this question since it depends on the language chosen by the parties and whether the parties intended the pension plan agreement to be part of the collective agreement or whether it has its own separate legal life.

It does provide an example of a situation where the parties must use clear and exact language to express what they have agreed upon.

In addition to what has been said, the parties may set out in their collective agreement the pension benefits paid for by the employer that must be paid to employees who retire during the life of the collective agreement. The obligation to provide pension benefits and the obligation to pay the premiums for such coverage are separate matters and both must be considered by the negotiators. On the other hand, the union might not be satisfied with this arrangement and might wish to participate in the administration of the pension plan. If this is the case, it would be necessary for the employer and the union to execute a pension agreement which outlines their respective obligations for providing and funding pension benefits for the employees who are covered, as well as the administrative mechanics of the plan.

If a dispute arises during the life of a collective agreement about whether a particular employee is entitled to a given form of welfare payment, for example, weekly indemnity benefits, the employer may take the position that it is the insurance carrier who determined the payment should not be made. The employer may argue that an employee who is refused benefits should look to the insurance carrier rather than to the employer for payment since the employer's obligation was limited to the payment of premiums only. It is just this kind of dispute that points up the need to be clear as to whether the employer's obligation is to pay premiums or provide benefits or both.

8. Termination

Each collective agreement — like this book — must ultimately come to an end. It will be recalled that the collective agreement must subsist for at least one year, but it may be for such longer period as the parties agree upon.

The termination article covers three different matters. The first is the date when the collective agreement becomes effective, that is, the date when the rights and obligations under the agreement start to run. It should be stressed that some portions of the collective agreement may become operative at different times. The wage article may, and often does, begin to run sooner than fringe benefits change under the same collective agreement.

The second item is the expiry date of the collective agreement. This must be clearly specified so it can be identified and applied. The third element is the period in which either party may give to the other notice to terminate or amend the collective agreement. The usual period selected is not more than three months or ninety days before the collective agreement expires and not less than two months or sixty days. An example of a termination article reads as follows:

This agreement shall become effective March 1, 1986, and shall continue in effect until February 29, 1988. It shall continue from year to year thereafter unless either party gives notice in writing to the other party not earlier than ninety (90) days or later than thirty (30) days prior to the date of expiration to terminate or renew this agreement or to negotiate a revision thereof.

A collective agreement may be signed on a date other than the effective date of its coming into operation. Many collective agreements are formally signed on a date after the date when the agreement begins to operate, although a short memorandum of settlement may have been executed when the negotiators reached an agreement they were prepared to recommend to their respective principals. Absent words in the agreement that specify some other date, the agreement will be considered to be in effect as of the date when it is signed.

Chapter 14

Conclusion

Having reviewed the process by which a collective agreement is negotiated and having looked at some of the more common provisions contained in collective agreements, it is time to conclude with some observations and some concerns about how well the art of collective bargaining is being practised in Canada.

Critics of collective bargaining, of whom there are many, do not argue that the process is entirely ineffective. Rather, the complaint is that the process is in need of improvement particularly because of its adversarial nature. There seems no doubt that collective bargaining, as with any process that requires negotiators to balance competing interests, can be improved and strengthened. While it is a generalization, it is also a fair statement that collective bargaining seems to work better in the private sector than in the public sector.

There are a number of reasons why this is so. The private sector has engaged in collective bargaining for a longer period of time than has the public sector and the parties, as well as their negotiators, have developed a higher level of sophistication in the use of effective and innovative collective bargaining techniques. Further, in the public sector there is often present the shadow, if not the person, of the government funding body which, while not a direct party to the bargaining, in the last analysis decides both price and priorities. This presence affects the bargaining dynamics for both the employer negotiators and the union representatives, creating complicated reporting and consultative procedures. From the employer's side, unless the lines of authority are clearly drawn and bargaining power is specifically delegated, there is confusion as to who in fact is controlling the negotiations and deciding the issues. From the union perspective, there is the frustration of bargaining with one group while another body, not present and reachable, is determining both the manner and the substance of the bargaining.

In the private sector the employer negotiators have direct control over the amount and method of payment of the funds available to the employer for collective bargaining. As we have seen, in many areas of the public sector the funds come from sources controlled by parties who are not at the bargaining table. This places the public sector employer in a straitjacket, by creating financial restrictions on what can be done even if the employer is persuaded it should be done. To complicate things, the restrictions may be the result of different financial priorities established by political considerations out of harmony with the administrative needs of the employer to provide a particular kind of service. Finally, and most fundamentally, the power relationship that exists in a rough sense in the private sector does not always apply in the public sector. Thus, the role of the outside agency can be used — or, more accurately, abused — to help one side or the other advance its bargaining objectives.

While these comments may help to explain some of the reasons why collective bargaining appears to be working better in the private than in the public sector, they do not address the root problems that apply to both sectors. In other words, to focus only on the distinctions between the two sectors ignores the collective bargaining fundamentals that apply to both.

The collective bargaining process is part of a continuing labour relations environment between an employer, a union and a group of employees. To a degree, the dynamics and tensions of the collective bargaining process are a mirror image of the employment community, and more broadly, of society in general.

The collective bargaining system, like the unions and employers that are part of it, has become somewhat structured and institutionalized. Unions have become powerful service businesses, providing bargaining and administrative services to their members for a fee, namely, the union dues. As the members of our society have become more polarized and fragmented, with a wide range of different priorities, a far larger demand on the union leadership has been generated to balance the different and often competing demands of the members. In addition, as many union leaders have discovered, the role of the union as an employer of its own staff and representatives is far different than acting as the spokesperson for the disadvantaged employees of another employer.

On the employer's side, some are indifferent in their outlook towards their employees, while others are engaged in what they believe is a holy crusade against unions. In these labour relations battles, the employees are placed between the hammer and anvil of the two antagonists. Even more to the point, a third institutional force — government — has a conflict between the role of acting as an employer and establishing collective bargaining examples and its role as mediator in the negotiations of others. This conflict is especially acute when some of the collective bargaining issues are the result of legislative initiatives, such as pay equity.

It is trite to observe that society in Canada has become fragmented and composed of increasing numbers of interest groups, whose vision of the world they want is radically opposite to each other. These groups, and the tensions between them, affect the collective bargaining process in a dramatic way. The very foundation of the theory of collective bargaining is that a union bargains on behalf of all the employees in a bargaining unit. This theory does not square with the present social scene, where a union is faced with vocal and competing groups within its own ranks, each of which has its own demands, some that cannot be reconciled and some directly in conflict. This divisiveness not only undercuts the orderly functioning of the bargaining process, but it also explains why many recommended memoranda of settlement are rejected in ratification meetings by the union membership.

Perhaps the expectations of all of us towards collective bargaining are unrealistically high. In view of the turmoil within our society, and the wide differences in the personal and institutional priorities legally harnessed together for bargaining purposes, it is little wonder that a consensus is difficult to reach at the bargaining table, especially when the issues involved are of such vital importance to the participants. After all, there is nothing more important to an individual employee than that person's job and the working conditions attached to it. Even more broadly, since many of the pressures on our society are largely consumer oriented, flowing from the proposition that we are, or should be, discontented with our present circumstances, it is surprising that the collective bargaining process is not more strained. The advertising urgings of what have been termed "the merchants of discontent" affect us all, and too many of us take out our frustrations at the bargaining table.

There is a deeper psychological reason for some of the present difficulties. Labour relations suffers from a surfeit of ideology. Certain employers are of the view that unions are evil institutions which have corrupted their innocent employees. These employers approach the bargaining table with no capacity to examine collective bargaining issues with reason or objectivity. Certain union representatives are equally committed to the ideological battle, and remain unconvinced that any employer has the least regard for the welfare and wellbeing of its employees. Unfortunately, echoes of class warfare, often torn out of a European context, sound across the bargaining terrain. These kinds of emotions, however genuine and deeply felt, can only deflect a negotiator, whose proper function is to represent others rather than advancing a personal cause.

Some parties to collective bargaining have tried to remake the world in their own image through collective bargaining obligations. For instance, some unions, out of a conviction for the protection of the environment, have made collective bargaining demands that prevent an employer from doing work in a certain way. The motive may be sincere and to many, socially desirable. The difficulty is that the collective bargaining process is not designed to accomplish things which can be better achieved through political actions since they affect all of society. Matters of general concern to the welfare of the community at large are best resolved by a consensus of the community, arrived at through political processes.

It is ironic that some parties to collective bargaining publicly decry the growing role of government in the process, while in practice the same parties have come to rely on government intervention at various stages in their own collective bargaining disputes. Thus, some parties have tailored their collective bargaining to fit the existence of conciliation and mediation and have become unable to resolve their own disputes by themselves. While there is nothing inherently wrong with this, it means that a third party — a government official — plays an increasingly important role in the settlement of a collective agreement. The resulting collective agreement is not a reflection of the necessary compromises of the two parties themselves, but bears a deepening government imprint, with a corresponding reduction in the responsibility for individual decision making. When the responsibility diminishes, so too does the capacity to make hard decisions, in the employment world and elsewhere.

A further point that must be made is that collective bargaining issues are not diminishing, in numbers of articles, subjects or complexity. One need only compare some of the collective agreements of twenty years ago with a current agreement between the same parties. It will be seen that not only have the comparable articles expanded remarkably in length, but there are many more issues, for example, occupational health and safety provisions, which are now part of these collective agreements. At the same time, many negotiators on both sides have not had an opportunity to expand their collective bargaining knowledge to reflect the new problems with which they must deal.

The labour relations community — and the people who work there — is as shifting and changeable as any other area of our society. Similarly, institutions are evolving in many directions, as evidenced by the outbreak of mergers, acquisitions and closures. Even the public sector is being forced to grapple with new priorities, impelled both by new social demands and competition for funds. All this brings instability and a need for negotiators who are both experienced and creative, people who have the imagination and capacity to find new solutions to issues that change so fast they are almost formless.

It is clear that little, if anything, can be done about some of these matters. Society will change as it will, and collective bargaining will be moulded and shaped by these changes. Nevertheless, there are some improvements in the process that bear consideration.

The first problem is the vacuum of information that often exists in a given collective bargaining situation. With the possible exception of the information supplied to participants in teachers' collective bargaining in Ontario, it is up to the parties themselves to provide their own research and data for bargaining. What is needed, and needed now, is an information bank to provide up-to-date collective bargaining information to employers and unions in all parts of the public and private sectors. While this would not magically resolve collective bargaining disputes, it would mean that the parties would be dealing with facts, rather than suppositions, and the information would be common to both sides. If both parties start from the same factual base, it is more likely they will be able to talk clearly and objectively about the issues.

The second concerns the role of government in the process. Labour relations confrontations often assume a high public profile, as they should. Acting in the public interest, governments in all jurisdictions have become more involved in the resolution of collective bargaining disputes. In many respects this government reaction is appropriate and necessary. Replacing boards of conciliation with mediation, for example, has been a success. Preventive mediation — that is, having experienced Ministry of Labour representatives meeting with the parties during the contract period to review how to better relate to each other — is another useful innovation. Yet, in other respects, the pendulum may have swung too far. Why, for instance, are applications for the appointment of a conciliation officer granted without regard to whether the parties have engaged in serious bargaining before the application was made? Why should the parties not be obliged to bargain in a meaningful way with each other, and to reach a bargaining impasse before the government steps in?

The difficulty is that some parties to collective bargaining have come to rely on government as a collective bargaining crutch, and have ducked the responsibility to make their own bargain. Perhaps there are times when government should step back and first require the parties to make every effort to settle their own problems by themselves. Conciliation should be more a last resort than a first bargaining step.

Another important problem involves the ratification process. The respective bargaining committees may negotiate together for many months before arriving at a basis of settlement. The resulting memorandum of settlement may cover dozens of individual items, and may be many pages in length. A collective agreement is not consummated until the parties obtain ratification from their respective principals, which, on the union's side, means the union members. It is unreasonable to expect that the membership can properly inform itself of the details of the proposed collective agreement, and vote intelligently, while attending a one or two-hour membership meeting. This is particularly the case where the vote in question is either "Yes" or "No", and a negative vote may be cast simply because of dissatisfaction with one narrow point in the overall proposed collective agreement.

As a consequence of these difficulties, some unions have tried to develop more effective ways to conduct ratification votes of members who are increasingly better educated and socially active. Unfortunately, there are other unions that do not seem to recognize that their membership is not monolithic and wants to participate directly in the ratification process to debate the merits of the various issues.

In jurisdictions such as Manitoba, a compulsory strike vote must be taken by the members of a bargaining unit before a lawful strike takes place. In other jurisdictions, there is no statutory requirement for a compulsory strike vote, although the matter is likely subject to the provisions of the union constitution. Some critics argue that if the Manitoba example were generally followed, it would ensure that employees had been given the opportunity to make their own decision to go on strike, even though in practice most unions will conduct their own strike vote to be sure that the membership is in support of strike action. In addition, it can be argued that consideration should be given to broadening the concept of a compulsory strike vote so that all the employees in the bargaining unit would have the right to cast a strike ballot, whether or not they were union members. In addition, the vote should be conducted and supervised by a neutral party, such as the appropriate Ministry of Labour. Another idea that could be considered is that the employer's last offer would be placed before the members of the bargaining unit, and the choice would be between acceptance of this offer or a decision to go on strike. The major advantage of this proposal would be to encourage the employer to make the best possible offer for settlement, in the hopes that it would be acceptable to the membership and make a strike unnecessary. In part, this concept has been adopted in Ontario, where an employer may make application to have a government-supervised secret ballot on the employer's last offer, either before or after a strike.

A further concern deals with a subject that is part of many collective bargaining confrontations — picketing. There is confusion in Canadian law as to the precise permissible limits of picketing. As a result, tense bargaining situations become more explosive because pickets do not have any guidelines to follow in a dispute. Thus, the relationship between the parties becomes inflamed, and the ultimate resolution of a dispute more difficult. The *Criminal Code* of Canada contains a large number of definitions of conduct that is unacceptable to society. However, the Code is so out of touch with the present realities of labour relations that it uses such archaic terms as "watching and besetting". There seems little doubt the law should be updated, and it should contain an outline of the means and form of lawful picketing in a labour relations dispute, and the sanctions to be applied in the event the law is breached.

Most of these suggestions, and others that could be made, are mechanistic, and can be resisted as being partisan or unworkable or both. Unfortunately, the thinking of many of us who are actively involved in the practical world of labour relations is too rigid and narrow. Yet the pressures to change are irresistible, if only because the consequences of bargaining failure are so high. The overriding issues that colour all collective bargaining are the social and economic troubles of our time. Our world is in a state of personal and group change, and the many voices of society ring out, loud, discordant and demanding. As economic circumstances worsen, as social goals change, as personal attitudes towards work and the workplace diverge, as interest groups coalesce, all these differently coloured threads must be woven into the fabric of collective bargaining. What we must recognize is that the bargaining table is where the fundamental compromises necessary to maintain a pluralistic society are being forged, and if the collective bargaining process becomes spent and impotent, we — all of us — will be the losers.

Index